Guerrilla Marketing in 30 Days

WORKBOOK

Fellow Guerrilla Marketers Speak Out . . .

Authors Jay Levinson and Al Lautenslager methodically explain strategies to help all businesses and organizations with their marketing. Spending 30 days with this book could be one of your more profitable actions this year.

—Jack Canfield, author, *Chicken Soup for the Soul*,
The Power of Focus, and *The Success Principles*

At last, a detailed step-by-step marketing program that doesn't take a lifetime to implement!

—Roger Parker, author, *Relationship Marketing for the
Internet, Web Design for Dummies*, and
www.onepagenewsletters.com.

Don't speed read *Guerrilla Marketing in 30 Days*. Read just one chapter in a sitting, no more, and then write down ideas that you can use to improve your business. Now read another chapter the next day and write down ideas. You'll find you'll implement some truly great ideas before you're halfway through the book. Try it.

—Jon Spoelstra, author,
Wall Street Journal bestseller, *Marketing Outrageously*

If you are strapped for cash as a small business, or a business professional and want to turbo-charge your marketing, read *Guerrilla Marketing in 30 Days*.

—Jeffrey J. Fox, best selling author of
How to Make Big Money in Your Own Small Business

Only Jay and Al can deliver on the promise to fix your marketing in 30 days. Buying this book and taking 30 days to turbo-charge your company is a no brainer.

—Guy Kawasaki, author, *The Art of the Start*
CEO, Garage Technology Ventures

Sunday	Monday	Tuesday	Wednesday	Thursday	Friday	Saturday
	1	2	3	4	5	6
7	8	9	10	11	12	13
14	15	16	17	18	19	20
21	22	23	24	25	26	27
28	29	30				

Guerrilla Marketing in 30 Days

WORKBOOK

Jay Conrad Levinson and Al Lautenslager

Ep Entrepreneur® Press

Editorial Director: Jere Calmes
Cover Design: Beth Hansen-Winter
Editorial and Production Services: CWL Publishing Enterprises, Inc., Madison, Wisconsin,
www.cwlpub.com

This publication is designed to provide accurate and authoritative information in regard to the
subject matter covered. It is sold with the understanding that the publisher is not engaged in ren-
dering legal, accounting, or other professional services. If legal advice or other expert assistance is
required, the services of a competent professional person should be sought.

—From a Declaration of Principles jointly adopted by
a Committee of the American Bar Association and
a Committee of Publishers and Associations

ISBN 1-59918-043-X

Printed in Canada

Contents

CONTENTS

Sunday	Monday	Tuesday	Wednesday	Thursday	Friday	Saturday
	1	2	3	4	5	6
7	8	9	10	11	12	13
14	15	16	17	18	19	20
21	22	23	24	25	26	27
28	29	30				

Using This Workbook

The number one challenge of entrepreneurs, business owners and managers is implementation. I see it all the time when I get involved in marketing coaching and consulting. I even see it when I speak to audiences. There are many who are great note takers, great readers and ask the right questions. Most then file the notes in the filing cabinet, put the books on the shelf and go right back to fighting the everyday "fires" of business. Implementation is "deprioritized" or totally absent.

In order to meet the challenges of implementation this workbook has been developed for you. The purpose of the workbook is to give you a road map, a step by step plan to guide your marketing activities throughout a whole plan year, a tracking device and a reference.

No this book is not a silver bullet. All plans take hard work. If you are challenged with hard work then you will be challenged with implementation. This book will serve as a fill in the blanks workbook and the guide for your planning process. It may not be all inclusive for you. Feel free to modify accordingly. You can even modify the wording in the electronically generated plan.

This is a unique tool for your marketing. Completing this workbook for the respective chapter of choice will turn into your plan. Using the program application that accompanies this workbook will give you the instant plan. Just fill out the workbook sections, answer the questions and with the push of a mouse button or an enter button on your computer you will have a ready to implement, totally presentable, easy to follow marketing plan. Your implementation challenge will be met head on.

We have tried to make it as easy as possible for you...but you have to totally put your mind to it. It requires deep thought, brainstorming, idea generation, prioritization, creativity and discipline. We don't teach those things here but we help you organized the results of them. We help you turn them into actionable steps so that you are not longer in the "most businesses fail to implement" category.

Hopefully you have the full text of *Guerrilla Marketing in 30 Days*. Can you complete this workbook and plan without it? Sure you can but your efforts will be much more enhanced using the main book as a reference tool.

Use the whole book for a very complete plan or pick and choose the sections that are right for your business. Your goal is just to do something. Let's work together to cross implementation off of your things to do list. Until you do that, Happy marketing!

DAY 1

Sunday	Monday	Tuesday	Wednesday	Thursday	Friday	Saturday
	1 ✔	2	3	4	5	6
7	8	9	10	11	12	13
14	15	16	17	18	19	20
21	22	23	24	25	26	27
28	29	30				

Marketing Mindset

THE GUERRILLA MARKETING mindset is dedicated to the proposition that each person and every activity in a company or organization should be focused daily on the question:

> ## How am I building awareness with my prospects and clients through all of our marketing?

While all employees, including entrepreneurial owners, know what their job is, they might not be able to even answer this one question about their mindset, in particular about their marketing mindset, let alone focus on it. If you want to be making many trips to the bank to make deposits, then all of the people in your organization must think like marketers in all that they do—starting with you.

It is more than manufacturing products or delivering services in the most cost-effective way. We've all heard it before: "Nothing happens until something gets sold." And nothing gets sold if no one out there knows about the product or service. Thinking like a marketer ensures this.

Marketing Mindset Inventory

1. How would you describe your current mindset, attitude, and beliefs as they relate to marketing?

_____

_____

_____

_____

2. Do you consciously think about this question: "How am I building awareness with my prospects and clients through all of our marketing?"

_____

_____

_____

_____

3. Rank your employees and co-workers on their marketing attitude and mindset related to the question in the item immediately preceding.

_____

_____

_____

_____

Marketing Philosophy Assessment

Complete these sentences.

1. I believe that the importance of marketing is:

_____

_____

2. This is what I think marketing will do for my business/organization:

_____

_____

Marketing Mindset Planner

1. How much time, effort, and thinking do you think marketing requires?

_____

_____

_____

_____

2. How much time are you willing to devote to your marketing overall? Per week? Per day? Per project?

_____

_____

_____

_____

_____

3. What will you do to make your marketing effective?

  ■ What will you do more of?

_____

_____

_____

  ■ What will you do less of?

_____

_____

_____

  ■ What will you start doing?

_____

_____

_____

  ■ What will you stop doing?

_____

_____

_____

Jumping the Hurdle

1. What factors might be blocking your marketing attitude, mindset, or effectiveness? (e.g., money, time, knowledge, staffing, creativity, discipline, etc.)

_____

_____

_____

Marketing Mindset Commitment

1. Write down your commitment to marketing. (e.g., "I know I get busy and so I have to raise my expectations about working on marketing. I will read, write, send, call, or say three to five things related to marketing every day.")

_____

_____

_____

_____

2. List three to five marketing things you can do each day before you start your daily routine. Choose from the list below. Check all that apply, but list and prioritize three to five here:

_____

_____

_____

_____

_____

❏ Handwrite a thank-you note to a prospect or customer.
❏ Enter names into a database.
❏ Brainstorm tagline ideas.
❏ Visit a competitor's Web site.
❏ Write an article.
❏ Make a list of press release ideas.

❏ Write a press release.

❏ Call a newspaper and ask who the feature editor is for your area of expertise.

❏ Write an e-mail sales letter.

❏ Call prospects and customers to get e-mail contact information.

❏ Write a series of survey questions.

❏ Brainstorm advertising concepts.

❏ Write a pitch letter to a radio or TV station.

❏ Get contact information from media outlets.

❏ Plan a renaming of your products.

❏ New product development and introduction.

❏ Invite a customer or prospect to your office for coffee or to discuss new ideas.

❏ Recognize a special prospect or customer.

❏ Discuss a fusion marketing idea with a strategic business partner.

❏ Read marketing-related Web sites.

❏ Post new information on your Web site.

❏ Plan your networking calendar for the week.

❏ Call to follow up on networking contacts.

❏ Get price estimates on printing and mailing for your direct mail campaign.

❏ Mail samples of your product to top prospects.

❏ Brainstorm ideas for an "enter to win" contest.

❏ Rewrite your on-hold message script.

❏ Write an article or paragraph for your newsletter.

❏ Brainstorm new product or service ideas.

❏ Plan a new customer service activity that truly delights customers.

❏ Celebrate successful marketing.

❏ Develop your benefit list and compare with those of your competitors.

❏ Develop a checklist, a top ten list, or something similar as a response to a marketing hook.

Guerrilla Hint

If you are still challenged with finding the right activities for the three to five things you've chosen, break your marketing down into general categories: Direct Mail, Networking, Publicity, Advertising, Fusion, Planning, New Products and Services, Marketing Communication Materials, etc. Concentrate on thinking up activities for one area at a time. No one is counting your "three to five things." The point here is to do something related to marketing every day to help you think about marketing all the time.

Day 1—Summary

- Marketing is everything you do or say that your prospects and customers see and hear from you.
- The marketing mindset is dedicated to the intention that each person and every activity in a company or organization should be focused daily on the following question: "How am I building awareness with my prospects and clients through our marketing?"
- If you want to succeed, you will need to think about your marketing all the time.
- Think about your marketing in the same way you think about paying your bills. You pay them routinely every month without giving them much thought.
- The first step in learning marketing skills is to develop a sensible attitude toward marketing—an attitude based on your beliefs, for what we believe determines how we behave.
- Your guerrilla marketing attitude combines optimism with energy so that marketing tasks are handled positively with enthusiasm and passion.
- Your marketing mindset is supported by your focus on the customer, focusing on their needs and doing everything possible to satisfy those needs.

Aha! Moments:

Next-Level Springboards, Notes, To-Do's, etc.

Sanity Check

❏ Is this too much or not enough activity?

❏ Am I comfortable with the processes described here, the workload, and the implementation?

❏ Will the expected outcomes take me to a new level?

Additional Notes

DAY 2

Sunday	Monday	Tuesday	Wednesday	Thursday	Friday	Saturday
	1	2 ✔	3	4	5	6
7	8	9	10	11	12	13
14	15	16	17	18	19	20
21	22	23	24	25	26	27
28	29	30				

The Purpose of Your Marketing

IF YOU DON'T KNOW WHERE you're going, how do you know when you get there? The same question can be asked about any journey, any vision, or any goal. The same question can be asked about guerrilla marketing and, more specifically, your marketing. How do you know how effective your marketing is if you don't know what you want it to accomplish for you? A guerrilla marketer knows what and where point B is. On Day 2 you are at point A. You know what's next: getting from point A to point B.

Devoting time and energy at the beginning of your planning process, along with setting your sights and defining the results expected of your marketing, will give you a far greater chance to make frequent trips to the deposit line of your favorite bank.

What results do you want your marketing to achieve?

What are your marketing goals and what is your marketing vision? Your marketing goals are nothing more than a statement of what results you want to achieve with your marketing. What is the primary reason you are marketing?

Marketing goals should fit into and support your overall business goals. Just like any other goals, marketing goals should be quantifiable and measurable and they must also be specific and realistic.

8

Business Goal-Setting Planner

One way to envision the goal-setting process and to achieve your goals is to look at goals you have achieved in the past. Look at how you achieved them and repeat the same or a similar process in working toward achieving new goals.

If, in the past, you have set and achieved marketing goals, make a list of them. These could be big marketing goals or smaller ones that led to bigger goals.

Marketing Goals Recently Achieved

- _____
- _____
- _____
- _____
- _____
- _____
- _____
- _____
- _____
- _____

If you cannot list specific marketing goals to analyze, list overall business goals recently achieved.

Overall Business Goals Recently Achieved

- _____
- _____
- _____
- _____
- _____
- _____
- _____
- _____
- _____
- _____

From either your marketing goals list or your overall business goals list above, identify the results from each goal achieved.

Results from Recently Achieved Goals

- _____
- _____
- _____
- _____
- _____
- _____
- _____
- _____
- _____
- _____

The point of understanding the purpose of your marketing and your marketing goals is to understand what type of company you strive to be, what you desire your future to be, where you are going both as a company and as a marketer. Since this is *Guerrilla Marketing in 30 Days* and not *Guerrilla Management in 30 Days*, concentrate on answering the following from a marketing perspective.

Marketing Goal-Setting Planner

What do you want your marketing to accomplish for your business? (e.g., an increase in sales dollars, a market share increase, a change in product or service mix, PR hits, identity awareness, an increase in profit dollars, etc.)

_____

_____

_____

_____

_____

_____

Roadblock Management Tool

You will hit roadblocks while pursuing your goals. Guerrilla marketers are flexible. This applies to achieving goals too. To prepare as much as possible for roadblocks, use this Roadblock Management Tool.

A little earlier you listed the marketing goals that you've achieved. You've probably also set goals that you did not achieve. For each goal unachieved, identify the roadblock or the reason that you did not achieve the goal.

Roadblock Identifier—Past

_____

_____

_____

_____

_____

What are some of the roadblocks that you anticipate will keep you from achieving your new marketing goals?

Roadblock Identifier—Future

_____

_____

_____

_____

_____

Vision Experiment

Define why you come to work every day. This should relate to your company and personal vision. If you can, state your vision here.

_____

_____

_____

What are you passionate about?

_____

_____

_____

What job duties do you like to perform?

_____

_____

_____

What job duties do you like to perform?

_____

_____

_____

Situational Analysis—Awareness Test

Comment on your awareness level in the marketplace.

_____

_____

_____

Does everyone that can buy from you know about you?

_____

Is awareness one of your goals? If so, are you thinking of activities to achieve your awareness goal?

_____

The Purpose of Your Marketing

How do you intend to get to where you want to be from where you are? While this question could lead to a thesis on business and marketing plans, that is not the intent here. This question is intended generally, to put your mind in the perspective of getting from point A to point B. It is not the details that count here, but rather the general attitudinal scope of your thinking. Here's an example: spending more time on the planning process; working as a planning group to brainstorm new products and service ideas; evaluating customer demands relative to what we deliver; building an infrastructure of equipment and people to deliver products and services to our niche in the marketplace.

Marketing Purpose List

How do you get business now? (Do people call you, visit you, order online, etc.?)

_____

_____

_____

How do you prefer to get business? (Do you want people to call you, visit you, order online, etc.?)

_____

_____

_____

Call-to-Action Inventory

What specific calls to action do these preferences translate into? (Call us today, Stop by our place of business now, Click here, etc.)

_____

_____

_____

_____

_____

Resource Manager

What resources (time, money, people, other) are required to reach your marketing goals?

_____

_____

_____

The End-in-Mind Test

For each of your goals, describe what success in achieving it will look like:

_____

_____

_____

_____

_____

_____

_____

_____

_____

_____

Day 2—Summary

- Devoting time and energy at the beginning of your planning process, along with setting your sights and defining the results expected of your marketing, will give you a far greater chance.

- Your marketing goals are nothing more than a statement of what results you want to achieve with your marketing.

- Marketing goals should fit into and support your overall business goals.

- A true guerrilla marketer knows that the selection and assortment of goals can be broad, but each individual goal must be specific, focused, and measurable.

- Guerrilla marketers set goals that can be met by creating an unmistakable path to the goals and benchmarks along the way to measure progress.

- Your marketing goals should be recorded, either written or logged into a computer.

- You have to accept the responsibility to proceed down your path, to generate activity that will achieve goals, and to hold yourself accountable.

Aha! Moments:

Next-Level Springboards:

Sanity Check

❏ Is this too much or not enough activity?
❏ Am I comfortable with the processes described here, the workload, and the implementation?
❏ Will the expected outcomes take me to a new level?

Additional Notes

DAY 3

Sunday	Monday	Tuesday	Wednesday	Thursday	Friday	Saturday
	1	2	3 ✔	4	5	6
7	8	9	10	11	12	13
14	15	16	17	18	19	20
21	22	23	24	25	26	27
28	29	30				

Competition/Research

LIKE IT OR NOT, COMPETITION IS ALL around us. In terms of free enterprise, competition is a good thing. In terms of a competitor eating your lunch, it is not so good. If the latter is the case, you must research your market and your competitors more to see what problems they are solving that you are not, what benefits they are offering that you are not, and what the marketplace awareness is for you compared with them.

> A guerrilla marketer knows everything going on in his or her marketplace, including information about leading prospects/customers and competitors.

One of the first steps of a guerrilla marketing attack is gaining knowledge. There are many forces that influence how customers purchase products and services, and there are many factors involved in their purchasing behavior. Gaining this knowledge goes a long way toward earning your designation as a guerrilla marketer.

Customer Research Analysis—Warm-Up

Note: The answers to these questions are not only a basis for your marketing plan; they are major components of your business model.

1. What problems do your customers have that they need solved?

_____

_____

_____

_____

2. How do they want them solved?

_____

_____

_____

_____

3. What is it worth to them to have their problems solved?

_____

_____

_____

_____

Primary Components of Research—Warm-Up

Note: Jot your immediate reactions to the questions below. Don't overanalyze at this point. Quick, initial thoughts are good.

1. What is being bought in your marketplace and where?

_____

_____

2. Who is buying what from whom?

_____

_____

3. Why do your customers buy the way they do?

_____

_____

4. How does what you know about current purchasing behavior predict future purchasing behavior?

_____

_____

5. What marketing, promotion, and/or advertising influences customers to buy?

_____

_____

6. What creates customer satisfaction?

_____

_____

7. What brands are your customers/prospects aware of?

_____

_____

8. What media/advertising reaches your customers best?

_____

_____

9. What price are your customers willing to pay?

_____

_____

10. What are the forecast marketing trends for your markets?

_____

_____

The "Big Three"

Asking prospects and customers these "big three" questions is a primary step in your market research:

1. What is your current supplier doing for you that you like?

_____

_____

_____

_____

2. What is your current supplier doing that you don't like?

_____

_____

_____

_____

3. If you could wave a magic wand and change things about your current supplier, what would you change?

_____

_____

_____

_____

Survey five customers and five prospects by telephone with the "big three" questions. Identify the customers and prospects here:

_____   _____

_____   _____

_____   _____

_____   _____

_____   _____

Competitor Research

1. List your top three competitors that you want to research.

_____

_____

_____

2. List the top three benefits of each competitor.

_____   _____   _____

_____   _____   _____

_____   _____   _____

3. List your top three benefits.

_____

_____

_____

4. Compare the competitors' benefits lists with yours.

_____

_____

_____

5. Describe how your company is unique compared with these competitors.

_____

_____

_____

6. Visit three competitive Web sites. Identify them here.

_____

_____

_____

7. Visit three competitive Web sites. Identify them here. Then answer the following questions for each Web site:

a. Does the company appear easy to do business with?

_____

_____

_____

b. How does its identity compare with yours?

_____

_____

_____

c. What is appealing? What is not?

_____

_____

_____

d. How can you make your Web site better as a result of this review?

_____

_____

_____

Competitor Comparison

1. Write down every reason you can think of to do business with your company.

_____

_____

_____

_____

_____

_____

2. Now do the same for your top competitors.

_____

_____

_____

_____

_____

_____

Now scratch off the reasons that you have in common with any of your competitors.

3. Are the remaining reasons good enough to be your competitive advantage?

_____

_____

_____

4. Do you need more? If so, identify thought starters for additional competitive advantages.

_____

_____

_____

Customer Feedback Summary

1. Summarize what customers want that competitors aren't providing.

_____

_____

_____

_____

_____

2. Summarize what customers are getting from competitors that they are not getting from you.

_____

_____

_____

_____

_____

_____

Research in Action

1. Buy something from two competitors online or offline. Document pros and cons.

_____   _____

_____   _____

_____   _____

_____   _____

_____   _____

_____   _____

Day 3—Summary

- At the same time as you research your marketing and your competitors, you must research your customers.

- A guerrilla marketer knows everything going on in his or her marketplace, including information about leading prospects/customers and competitors.

- Market research is a critical component in the overall business planning process.

- The only way to know that you have a competitive advantage is to know what the competition has and does not have.

- Market research and competitive intelligence anticipates emerging threats and uncovers opportunities.

- A guerrilla marketer knows who the ideal customers are and what the competition is doing to go after them.

Aha! Moments:

Next-Level Springboards, Notes, To-Do's, etc.

Sanity Check

❏ Is this too much or not enough activity?

❏ Am I comfortable with the processes described here, the workload, and the implementation?

❏ Will the expected outcomes take me to a new level?

Additional Notes

DAY 4

Sunday	Monday	Tuesday	Wednesday	Thursday	Friday	Saturday
	1	2	3	4 ✔	5	6
7	8	9	10	11	12	13
14	15	16	17	18	19	20
21	22	23	24	25	26	27
28	29	30				

Target Market

MARKETING BOILS DOWN TO a point where it is easy to market if you know what to market and whom to target. The last part of this statement is more than half of marketing. The right marketing of the right products to the wrong target is like a hunter shooting into the wind without hitting anything.

Targeting involves determining who buys what, why they buy it, and where they buy it. Identifying these factors is essential to your marketing and to using your resources as efficiently as possible.

> Analyze the profiles of your most successful accounts.
> Then, devise a plan to reach potential customers
> who share those traits.

The key to targeting is planning ahead. Start by asking, "Who will benefit the most from my products and services?" Begin building a detailed profile of your current customers. Why do they do business with you? What do they have in common? How can you best service their current and future needs? Then think about the "perfect customer." If you could magically create the "ideal client," what would he or she look like?

Narrow your target, create a niche, and sell to it aggressively.

Target Market—Preliminary Direction

Who will benefit the most from your company's products and services?

1. Types of companies:

_____

_____

_____

_____

2. Specific companies that come to mind:

_____

_____

_____

_____

Target Market Identification

Begin building a detailed profile of your current customers.
If you have customers now, describe each of the target market attributes for the majority of them.

1. Characteristics:

_____

_____

_____

_____

2. Habits:

_____

_____

_____

_____

3. Activity:

_____

_____

_____

_____

4. Desires:

_____

_____

_____

_____

5. Geography:

_____

_____

_____

_____

6. Why do your customers do business with you? Think benefits!

_____

_____

_____

_____

Niche Identification

Can you break these target markets down into even smaller segments?

_____

_____

_____

_____

Target Market Magic Wand Exercise

1. If you could magically create the "ideal client," what would he or she look like?

_____

_____

_____

_____

_____

2. What other prospects that you know of share this profile?

_____

_____

_____

_____

_____

3. What characteristics, habits, activity, desires, or geography do you need to address to appeal to the prospects you've identified above?

_____

_____

_____

_____

_____

4. What trends related to your target market will you have to address with your business, products, or services? How can you best service your target market's current and future needs?

_____

_____

_____

_____

_____

Target Market Definition

Based on the above characteristics, desires, activity, and geography, write out your target market definition.

_____

_____

_____

_____

_____

Day 4—Summary

- It is easy to market if you know what to market and whom to market.

- When it comes to target marketing, aim all activities as specifically as possible.

- Targeting involves determining who buys what, why they buy it, and where they buy it.

- You have to know to whom you want to sell your products and services before you can successfully zero in on them with your marketing efforts.

- By identifying how you got your current customers, you can create more efficient marketing strategies that hit your target more accurately.

Aha! Moments:

Next-Level Springboards, Notes, To-Do's, etc.

Sanity Check

❑ Is this too much or not enough activity?

❑ Am I comfortable with the processes described here, the workload, and the implementation?

❑ Will the expected outcomes take me to a new level?

Additional Notes

DAY 5

Sunday	Monday	Tuesday	Wednesday	Thursday	Friday	Saturday
	1	2	3	4	5 ✔	6
7	8	9	10	11	12	13
14	15	16	17	18	19	20
21	22	23	24	25	26	27
28	29	30				

Positioning

YOUR MARKETING REQUIRES POSITIONING for success. Positioning is considered one of the core elements of marketing strategy. Positioning is more than a catchy tagline or a heavily promoted feature or brand, although a tagline will help. It is more than being at the right place at the right time and it is more than having a crack sales team (although any of these can cause a one-time windfall of profits). Positioning actually is a base upon which all other marketing builds toward the goal of better relationships with a target market.

Positioning is truly what your business will stand for in the minds of your prospects and customers.

Positioning is more than clever manipulation of a market's perception. It truly is a statement of your company or organization's true identity and true value to a target market.

A well-thought-out positioning statement defines a company's vision and direction. It describes:

- Who you really are as a company
- What business you are really in
- Who exactly buys your product and services
- Product and service demands by your market
- Competitive advantages and unique value offered by you

33

Position Measurement Checklist

In *Guerrilla Marketing*, third edition, it states that when you have clearly focused on your markets, you can clarify a market position. This focus should measure the position against the four criteria below.

1. Does my position offer a benefit that my target market really wants? Y ❑ N ❑
2. Is it an honest-to-goodness benefit and not a feature? Y ❑ N ❑
3. Does the benefit truly distinguish me from my competitors? Y ❑ N ❑
4. Is the benefit unique or difficult to copy? Y ❑ N ❑

If you answered no to any of the four questions, consider the following questions.

1. What benefit could you offer that people in your target market really, really want?

_____

_____

_____

_____

2. What can you offer people in your target market that makes them feel better, helps them avoid pain, saves them time, and saves them money?

_____

_____

_____

_____

3. What benefit can you offer that competitors cannot?

_____

_____

_____

_____

4. What benefit could you offer that competitors could not copy?

_____

_____

_____

_____

A Tagline for You!

Brainstorm taglines of 10 words or less. Here are some examples:

- For an appliance store: "We cook it, clean it, and chill it"
- For a financial planner: "Building Your Future Dreams"
- For a health insurance agent: "Taking Care of You When You Need It Most"
- For a local delivery service: "On their desk, Out of your hands"
- For a professional organizer: "Places, spaces, and peace of mind"

To generate taglines, list adjectives or verbs that relate to your business, products, or services. Mix and match combinations and brainstorm ideas. Then, share your ideas with friends and get their input and ideas. Brainstorm more combinations. Do this exercise every other day. If you continue doing it, your tagline will come to you when you least expect it.

Adjectives	**Verbs**
_____	_____
_____	_____
_____	_____
_____	_____
_____	_____
_____	_____

Combinations and Brainstorms

_____

_____

_____

_____

_____

Competitive Positioning Analysis

List competitors that you know of that:

1. Were first:

■ to market with a product, service, or idea.

_____

_____

_____

_____

■ have a great sales force.

_____

_____

_____

_____

■ to just get lucky.

_____

_____

_____

_____

2. Do these competitors have a real position or positioning strategy, or do they just rely on the above factors?

_____

_____

_____

_____

Positioning Perception Exercise

What is your perception and the market perception of the following products and how would you characterize the positioning of each of them?

1. Pepsi

_____

_____

2. Ford Truck

_____

_____

3. Sony

_____

_____

4. Your local chiropractor

_____

_____

5. Your local florist

_____

_____

6. Your favorite pizza delivery service

_____

_____

7. Your local dry cleaner

_____

_____

8. One of your favorite vendors

_____

_____

Why is that vendor one of your favorites? Is that reason related to their positioning?

_____

_____

_____

_____

Positioning Statement Generator

1. Fill in the blanks:

I represent a _____ company and work with _____ who want to

improve/increase their _____ by _____.

2. What is the number-one thing you want your customers to know and remember about you?

_____

_____

_____

_____

3. Write out your position statement.

_____

_____

_____

_____

_____

_____

_____

_____

Day 5—Summary

- Your marketing requires positioning for success.

- Positioning is more than a catchy tagline or a heavily promoted feature or brand.

- A position is how you are perceived in the minds of your prospects and customers.

- Positioning strategies must have amazing clarity.

- Once you have a crystal-clear positioning statement, communicating to your target market becomes easier.

- Market positioning is a promise from you to your target market.

Aha! Moments:

Next-Level Springboards, Notes, To-Do's, etc.

Sanity Check

❑ Is this too much or not enough activity?

❑ Am I comfortable with the processes described here, the workload, and the implementation?

❑ Will the expected outcomes take me to a new level?

Additional Notes

DAY 6

Sunday	Monday	Tuesday	Wednesday	Thursday	Friday	Saturday
	1	2	3	4	5	6 ✔
7	8	9	10	11	12	13
14	15	16	17	18	19	20
21	22	23	24	25	26	27
28	29	30				

Niche Marketing

A NICHE MARKET IS SIMPLY A VERY specific portion of a much larger target market. Niche marketing allows you to target a very specific group of customers and give them exactly what they want and need.

Take, as an example, a target market niche that needs marketing consulting. Marketing consulting is a broad target market. Direct mail consulting, PR consulting, and strategic marketing planning are three niches within the broader target market.

> A niche market is a limited, crystal-clear range of products or services sold to a tightly focused target group, whose members all have particular wants and needs served by the niche products and services.

The point to be taken from this is to focus, serve what you serve best, and prosper accordingly. And prosper you will if you are niched. A target market that is too broad causes inefficiencies, higher costs, and underdeveloped customer service and attention. Narrowing a focus creates a better environment for success, an opportunity to stand out, to be an expert, and to be at the top of your customers' or prospects' minds for your niched product or service area.

Niche Comparison

Pick three markets and list the leader in each of the three markets.

Market	Market Leader

1. What unique things related to product, service, or customer satisfaction are present for these leaders?

   _____

   _____

   _____

   _____

2. What special things do you do that your competitors do not do?
   For example:
   ❑ Remember names, kid's names, birthdays
   ❑ Smile
   ❑ Give something away
   ❑ Bail out a customer's emergency; go the extra mile
   ❑ Say thank you
   ❑ Offer a cordial greeting
   ❑ Call to follow up
   ❑ Call for any reason
   ❑ Send a reminder and/or a thank-you note
   ❑ Refer
   ❑ Find a hard-to-find product or service for the customer

   _____

   _____

   _____

   _____

Marketing to Your Niche

1. Who are some of the top decision-makers in your identified niche (by title or name, if you have them)?

_____

_____

_____

_____

2. Who are some of the key editors and reporters for publications serving your niche?

_____

_____

_____

_____

Niche Identification

1. What problems, complaints, irritations, and hassles are you hearing from your target market that might identify a niche opportunity for you?

_____

_____

_____

_____

2. What are you doing that your customers like?

_____

_____

_____

_____

3. What are you doing that your customers don't like? (Fix these things immediately.)

_____

_____

_____

_____

4. Could competitors do something better than you—like not doing those things your customers don't like about you? (See question above.)

_____

_____

_____

_____

5. What can you add to your product and service that your competitors don't have, don't do, or can't do?

_____

_____

_____

_____

6. Can you bundle products and services or something else?

_____

_____

_____

_____

7. What can you do to make your product or service more convenient to your customers?

_____

_____

_____

_____

8. What can you do that is extreme—fastest, best, largest, most convenient, etc.?

_____

_____

_____

_____

9. What can you make that will last longer for your customers?

_____

_____

_____

_____

10. What can you offer that will save time, save money, or be less hassle for your customers?

_____

_____

_____

_____

11. How would you define your niche market?

_____

_____

_____

_____

Day 6—Summary

- "Everybody" is not a target market. "Everybody" is also not a niche.

- A niche market is simply a very specific portion of a much larger target market.

- Narrowing a focus creates more of an environment for success, an opportunity to stand out, to be an expert, and to be at the top of your customers' or prospects' minds for your niched product or service area.

- When considering the different target markets that you operate in, you must consider what you offer that's different.

- If you don't have differences, you must find them, develop them, or create them.

- Niche strategies are developed and evolve because a particular target market need or demand is not satisfied.

- Finding your niche will give you an identity that your competitors don't have.

Aha! Moments:

Next-Level Springboards, Notes, To-Do's, etc.

Sanity Check

❏ Is this too much or not enough activity?

❏ Am I comfortable with the processes described here, the workload, and the implementation?

❏ Will the expected outcomes take me to a new level?

Additional Notes

DAY 7

Sunday	Monday	Tuesday	Wednesday	Thursday	Friday	Saturday
	1	2	3	4	5	6
7 ✔	8	9	10	11	12	13
14	15	16	17	18	19	20
21	22	23	24	25	26	27
28	29	30				

Marketing Plan and Strategy

WHILE ALL OF THE 30 DAYS of this *Guerrilla Marketing* workbook will contribute to your overall marketing plan, this Day covers tips, tactics, and techniques related to that plan.

Your market plan boils down to developing your roadmap. What paths will you take, which turns will you make, and, most important of all, where you are going? Unless you have an endpoint on your road map, how do you know which path to take? In the words of the immortal Yogi Berra, "You got to be very careful if you don't know where you're going because you might not get there."

> A plan, and the ultimate result of this 30-day process, offers a simple strategy or set of strategies, a marketing calendar, an evaluation system, and a selection of weapons and tactics that give you complete control of your marketing.

A good plan conveys your company's vision to target markets, customers, and employees. As part of this vision, your plan should emphasize your company's long-term goals and the path to get there. Stops along the journey, in the form of initiatives and actions, are key landmarks on the roadmap to executing the plan.

Marketing Plan Sanity Check

1. Do you feel that you know your market inside and out, including what customers want and expect?   Y ❑ N ❑

2. If no, what additional information do you need for effective planning?

   _____

   _____

   _____

3. What is hindering you from satisfying customers, e.g., competitors, barriers to entry, costs, outside influences, budgets, knowledge, etc.?

   _____

   _____

   _____

   _____

   _____

4. What items from the above answers can you plan to attack and prioritize?

   _____

   _____

   _____

Note: The outcome of this Day will be your total planning perspective. All of the components of the plan listed for this Day are covered in separate Days. Each Day is as important as the others toward creating your overall marketing plan. Developing that plan will take more than one Day.

Planning Activity Plan

1. What portion of each day will you devote to reviewing your plan and any necessary revising?

   _____

   _____

   _____

2. How often will you review your plan?

   _____

   _____

3. Write a hypothetical outcome statement about the completion of your plan. Here's an example:

   After planning to increase leads and referrals for our sales staff to pursue and convert, many marketing weapons were employed. Utilizing the guerrilla marketing resources of time, energy, and imagination, we embarked on an aggressive PR campaign, issuing press releases for new services introduced, new information available demonstrating our expertise, and announcements of events for our target market to sample the service. This was backed up with "meet and greet" programs at various networking events, ads in trade association directories, and telemarketing to trade-show attendees. The leads generated were focused, open to our follow-up, and ripe for conversion. We ended up getting more leads than our sales force could follow up on, so we implemented a telemarketing inside sales force. Conversion increased, sales increased, and we made more trips to the bank to make deposits.

   _____

   _____

   _____

   _____

   _____

   _____

   _____

   _____

   _____

Ready, Set, Go ... Ready, Aim, Fire ... Ready, Plan, Implement

1. List and prioritize your marketing planning objectives, e.g.:
- Introduce product or service
- Position company, product, or service as a market leader
- Counteract competitive strategy
- Generate leads and get referrals
- Obtain market share in a new geographical area
- Renew, refresh, and communicate new identity

Your list:

_____

_____

_____

_____

_____

_____

_____

2. Outline your plan. Start with the eight components described on this Day (below). Take the eight steps and develop plan subheadings, supplemental information, and new ideas.

- Purpose of your marketing

_____

_____

_____

_____

- Target market

_____

_____

_____

_____

■ Niche

_____
_____
_____
_____

■ Benefits/competitive advantage

_____
_____
_____
_____

■ Identity

_____
_____
_____
_____

■ Marketing weapons

_____
_____
_____
_____

■ Marketing budget

_____
_____
_____
_____

- What's next to think about?

_____

_____

_____

_____

3. What information (research) do you still need?

_____

_____

_____

_____

4. Where and how will you obtain that information?

_____

_____

_____

_____

Day 7—Summary

- Once you understand your company to its fullest, the dynamics of the marketplace, and how to identify shifts, trends, and changes, you are ready to plan.

- A good manager will see a marketing plan as important as a financial plan or a management plan.

- A plan, and the ultimate result of this 30-day process, offers a simple strategy or set of strategies, a marketing calendar, an evaluation system, and a selection of weapons and tactics that give you complete control of your marketing.

- A good plan conveys your company's vision to target markets, customers, and employees.

- Planning is the first phase of guerrilla marketing, followed quickly by launching the marketing and then maintaining the marketing.

- A marketing plan can be developed with seven sentences, addressing each of the following components:

  — The purpose of your marketing (see Day 2)

- Target market (see Day 4)
- Niche (see Day 6)
- Benefits/competitive advantage (see Day 8)
- Identity (see Day 9)
- Marketing weapons (various days)
- Marketing budget (see Day 25)

- One of the benefits of the marketing plan is it forces you to think and rethink your marketing.
- A marketing plan is a "job manual" for attracting potential customers and turning them into paying customers.

Aha! Moments:

Next-Level Springboards, Notes, To-Do's, etc.

Sanity Check

❏ Is this too much or not enough activity?

❏ Am I comfortable with the processes described here, the workload, and the implementation?

❏ Will the expected outcomes take me to a new level?

Additional Notes

DAY 8

Sunday	Monday	Tuesday	Wednesday	Thursday	Friday	Saturday
	1	2	3	4	5	6
7	8 ✔	9	10	11	12	13
14	15	16	17	18	19	20
21	22	23	24	25	26	27
28	29	30				

Competitive Advantage and Benefits

THE ONE QUESTION ASKED BY the prospect is "What's in it for me?" That's the mantra of the prospect. "How is whatever you are saying, doing, selling, or marketing a benefit to me?" The key word here is *benefit*. Notice that the word *feature* was not used. Many marketers and sales people confuse *features* with *benefits*.

Prospects don't care about you. They care about themselves and anything they have to read or listen to that is not related to them is of little or no interest.

A feature is a factual statement about a product or service. Factual statements aren't why customers buy. Benefits are the reason. Features are things that might be included in the "About Us" section of a Web site.

Benefits sell. Benefits clearly answer the customer's question of "What's in it for me?" or "What results will I get that will improve my current situation?" or "Will it make me healthier, wealthier, or wiser?" Ben Franklin was a benefits kind of guy.

The most compelling benefits are those that provide emotional or financial return. It's not the steak, it's the sizzle. It's not the gift, it's the thought. It's not the price, it's the overall value. Emotional returns are related to making the customer feel better in some way. Financial returns generally save money or make money for a customer.

56

Feature List Generation

List at least five features of your product or service: what do you have that is the biggest, the quickest, the cheapest, the most up-to-date technologically, the friendliest, etc.?

    1. We have the largest _____ in the industry.

    2. Our _____ is the quickest around.

    3. We provide the cheapest _____ for our customers.

    4. Our _____ process is the most up-to-date technologically.

    5. We pride ourselves in having the most user-friendly _____.

    6. _____

    7. _____

    8. _____

    9. _____

    10. _____

Benefit List Generation

For each of the features that you generated above, state what that feature can do for the customer: e.g., saves them time, saves them money, makes them money, makes them healthier, keeps their inventory low, tastes better to them, is less filling for them, etc.

    1. _____

    2. _____

    3. _____

    4. _____

    5. _____

    6. _____

    7. _____

    8. _____

    9. _____

    10. _____

What can you do, what problem can you solve, or what can you offer for customers that no one else can?

1. _____
2. _____
3. _____
4. _____

What can you do, what problem can you solve, or what can you offer for customers that no one else can?

1. _____
2. _____
3. _____
4. _____

What can your competitors solve, offer, or do that you cannot?

1. _____
2. _____
3. _____
4. _____

Now from the above information, create your benefits list. For example, "parking spaces closer to the door so you don't have to walk as far" may be a benefit of a senior medical supplies store that doesn't always show up on the benefit list.

1. _____
2. _____
3. _____
4. _____
5. _____
6. _____
7. _____
8. _____
9. _____
10. _____

Customer Feedback Mechanism

Ask customers to identify your true benefits and record them here.

1. _____
2. _____
3. _____
4. _____
5. _____
6. _____
7. _____

What complaints and inquiries have you heard from customers and prospects that may uncover a need that the right benefit could satisfy?

1. _____
2. _____
3. _____
4. _____
5. _____
6. _____
7. _____

Are any of these complaints and inquiries within your company? Y ❏ N ❏

1. _____
2. _____
3. _____
4. _____
5. _____

From this benefits list above, list prospects who might be interested in each: e.g., "Brubaker and company would be interested in a quicker delivery time because they have too much inventory already."

_____

_____

_____

_____

_____

Competitive Advantage

List your competitors' benefits:

1. _____

2. _____

3. _____

4. _____

5. _____

6. _____

7. _____

What benefit(s) do you offer that your competitors don't?

1. _____

2. _____

3. _____

Prepare a written description of your competitive advantage for all employees, salespeople, and customers.

_____

_____

_____

_____

_____

Day 8—Summary

- The mantra of the prospect is "How is whatever you are saying, doing, selling, or marketing a benefit to me?"

- A feature is a factual statement about a product or service. Factual statements aren't why customers buy. Benefits are the reason.

- Benefits sell. Benefits clearly answer the customer's question, "What's in it for me?"

- The most compelling benefits are those that provide emotional or financial return.

- A benefit will improve the life, finances, health, or well-being of someone.

- A benefit that you offer that competitors don't is a unique benefit and a competitive advantage.

- Creating an advantage that is difficult to duplicate is gaining the ultimate competitive advantage.

- Asking your customers why they do business with you will help you identify your competitive advantages.

Aha! Moments:

Next-Level Springboards, Notes, To-Do's, etc.

Sanity Check

❑ Is this too much or not enough activity?

❑ Am I comfortable with the processes described here, the workload, and the implementation?

❑ Will the expected outcomes take me to a new level?

Additional Notes

DAY 9

Sunday	Monday	Tuesday	Wednesday	Thursday	Friday	Saturday
	1	2	3	4	5	6
7	8	9 ✔	10	11	12	13
14	15	16	17	18	19	20
21	22	23	24	25	26	27
28	29	30				

Identity and Branding

THERE ARE A FEW COMMON CHARACTERISTICS of successful identities. First, the identity needs to be clear and free of confusion. A confused customer is not a customer for long. There should be no confusion as to who you are. A consistent identity is a successful identity, the same identity, everywhere, over and over. Change the identity and you change customer perceptions. Change perceptions and you collapse your marketing.

> The consistent use of your company's identity is critical to effective marketing communication and the eventual building of your company, product, service, or brand awareness.

An identity plays a part in grabbing attention, getting interest, creating desire, and causing action—all the purposes of successful marketing and marketing communication programs.

Your brochure, your presentation folders, your ads, your letterhead, and your business cards, not to mention your products and services, all represent your identity. Your identity is one of the most valuable and one of the most controllable assets your company has.

Because it is so valuable, you should take the right amount of time to make sure that the identity is clear and consistent and has the "personality" you want it to have.

Identity Word Association

Write down ten adjectives, any adjectives.

1. _____
2. _____
3. _____
4. _____
5. _____
6. _____
7. _____
8. _____
9. _____
10. _____

Now think of one company—local or national, business-to-business or consumer—that comes to mind for each adjective.

1. _____
2. _____
3. _____
4. _____
5. _____
6. _____
7. _____
8. _____
9. _____
10. _____

Write down why you make this association or what makes you remember it most: experience, advertisement, radio, referral, TV, delivery truck, billboard, sign, etc.

1. _____
2. _____
3. _____
4. _____
5. _____
6. _____
7. _____
8. _____
9. _____
10. _____

List five consumer products and five products or services that are sold business-to-business. What do you remember about each one? What made you remember each one? (See association examples above.)

Consumer Products

1. _____
2. _____
3. _____
4. _____
5. _____

Business-to-Business Products or Services

1. _____
2. _____
3. _____
4. _____
5. _____

Now list one-word adjectives that describe you, your business, and your products and services. Quantity is not the key; razor-sharp adjectives are.

1. _____

2. _____

3. _____

4. _____

5. _____

Which of the adjectives listed above do you want people to remember and know you for?

1. _____

2. _____

3. _____

4. _____

5. _____

How can you incorporate your new adjectives into your identity?

_____

_____

_____

_____

_____

_____

_____

_____

_____

_____

_____

_____

Developing the Identity Standard

One component of an *identity audit* is collecting marketing communication materials that feature the corporate identity (brochures, business cards, letterheads, advertisements, signage, Web site, etc.). Once collected, these are all inspected (audited) to see how the identity is used. Typically, numerous variations of the identity will be found. This is usually because no one knows how the various components of the identity should be used: there is no standard.

1. Describe the "look and feel" of your identity.

_____

_____

_____

_____

2. List all the places where your identity is used.

_____

_____

_____

_____

3. Where is there inconsistent use of your identity in the items listed above, e.g., letterhead, business cards, signage, Web site, delivery vehicle, logo apparel, etc.?

_____

_____

_____

_____

4. Cite some standards for the use of your identity, e.g., color, size, fonts, application, design, etc.

_____

_____

_____

_____

Branding the Identity

1. What promise does your brand make?

_____

_____

_____

_____

2. Are you keeping the promise? Y ❏ N ❏

3. Does your brand evoke an emotional response? Y ❏ N ❏

4. Does your brand represent or communicate a particular company or corporate culture? Y ❏ N ❏

5. What could be changed about your identity to update it?

_____

_____

_____

_____

Summary

- Who you are and what you do are the basis of all your marketing.

- Part of your identity is your primary marketing message.

- Identity is everything customers or prospects see and hear about you and what they remember about you.

- Identity is based on truth and honesty. Image is many times phony and something that the company is not.

- Identity must be clear and free of confusion.

- Identity is the accumulation of all visual elements of a company's communication to the outside world.

- Branding is also the foundation of your communication effort.

- Branding creates emotional bonding to a product, a service, a company, or an identity.

- The brand must be different.

- Your brand is a promise. Make sure you deliver on what your brand promises.

Aha! Moments:

Next-Level Springboards, Notes, To-Do's, etc.

Sanity Check

❏ Is this too much or not enough activity?

❏ Am I comfortable with the processes described here, the workload, and the implementation?

❏ Will the expected outcomes take me to a new level?

Additional Notes

DAY 10

Sunday	Monday	Tuesday	Wednesday	Thursday	Friday	Saturday
	1	2	3	4	5	6
7	8	9	10 ✔	11	12	13
14	15	16	17	18	19	20
21	22	23	24	25	26	27
28	29	30				

Marketing Communication and Creative Planning

BY THIS DAY YOU HAVE IDENTIFIED your benefits and competitive advantages. You know who your target prospects and customers are and what they want. Now you have to communicate these benefits and advantages to your prospects and customers. You need to communicate your advantages in a compelling and convincing way. You have to articulate your message well and state it often. You do this through the many marketing avenues available for communication. All of this falls under the heading of "marketing communication." You have to get the word out.

> Marketing communication communicates product characteristics, benefits, and everything about your business and the people associated with it.

Marketing communication takes all of these guerrilla-marketing elements and blends them into a strategy that totally reflects the identity that you learned on Day 9. The communication strategy forms and directs all of your communication and the subsequent development of your marketing communication materials.

71

Clarity Connector

Clarity is just one of the primary considerations when developing your marketing materials.

1. How focused are your message and communication on what your prospect receives—not what you do, not who you are, and not how long you have been in business? The message should be about benefits: "What's in it for me, the prospect?"

_____

_____

_____

_____

2. Does your message provide enough content and information to persuade?

_____

_____

_____

_____

3. How would you consider the layout and the look of your marketing communications material?

_____

_____

_____

_____

4. Are you using credibility mechanisms—e.g., testimonials, case studies, correct grammar, zero typos—in your marketing communications?

_____

_____

_____

_____

Marketing Materials—Usage Analysis

1. How are your marketing materials used?

   Information sent in response to a prospect's inquiry. Y ❑ N ❑

   A mailing to a targeted group of prospects to keep in touch. Y ❑ N ❑

   Information for prospect appointments as a talking piece or a leave-behind piece. Y ❑ N ❑

   Postings on a Web site or developed as content for a Web page. Y ❑ N ❑

   A handout in your place of business for walk-in customers to pick up: "Take One." Y ❑ N ❑

   An enclosure with proposals for your products and services. Y ❑ N ❑

   An enclosure with your product packaging. Y ❑ N ❑

Marketing materials typically are best used to inform, educate, and sell those who have already expressed an interest in your services.

Creative Planning

Creative Plan Points to Consider

1. Is the marketing communication directed to the right target market? Y ❑ N ❑

   What makes you think that?

   _____

   _____

   _____

   _____

2. Are you communicating from the perspective of "What's in it for me, the prospect?"
Y ❏ N ❏

What makes you think that?

_____

_____

_____

_____

3. Does the "look and feel" reflect who you really are and is it consistent with other marketing communication? Y ❏ N ❏

What makes you think that?

_____

_____

_____

_____

4. Do you continually evaluate your marketing communications in terms of changing customer demands, competitive actions, or new products and services? Y ❏ N ❏

Comment on your answer.

_____

_____

_____

_____

5. Are you thinking about how much money you are spending or how much you could get in return if your investment in marketing communication works? Y ❏ N ❏

Comment on your answer.

_____

_____

_____

_____

6. Are you communicating frequently enough? Y ❑ N ❑

   Comment on how you know you are or what you think you need to do in terms of frequency:

   _____

   _____

   _____

   _____

Marketing Communication Piece Planner

List the marketing communication pieces planned for the year. (You may want to revise this after going through the creative strategy process practice below.)

_____

_____

_____

_____

_____

_____

_____

Creative Strategy Process Practice

Pick five communication vehicles from this list:

letters	signage	brochures	envelopes
faxes	billboards	postcards	letterhead
Web site	delivery vehicle	newsletter	packaging
press kits	speeches	presentations	videos
trade show booths	business cards	on-hold messages	other

List them here:

_____

_____

_____

_____

Write out the three components of the creative strategy for each one chosen.

1. _____

_____

_____

2. _____

_____

_____

3. _____

_____

_____

4. _____

_____

_____

5. _____
_____
_____

Marketing Communication Planning Outline Worksheet

Outline the various sections (text, graphics, layout, design, etc.) of each one of your marketing communication materials.

1. _____
_____
_____

2. _____
_____
_____

3. _____
_____
_____

4. _____
_____
_____

5. _____
_____
_____

How will you evaluate the effectiveness of each of each marketing communication piece: number of calls, returned cards, Web site hits, etc.?

_____

_____

_____

_____

Usage Test

1. Which one marketing communication piece do you use the most?

_____

_____

_____

2. Which one marketing communication piece do you use the least?

_____

_____

_____

3. Which marketing communication pieces do your prospects like or respond to the most?

_____

_____

_____

_____

Budget Check

1. If budget were not an issue, which marketing communication would you put into place?

_____

_____

_____

_____

2. If marketing budget is an issue, which one marketing communication piece will you put into place?

_____

_____

_____

_____

Bang for Your Buck

1. In which different ways can you use your marketing communication pieces, e.g., direct mail, handouts, posted on a Web site, dropped from a helicopter, etc.?

_____

_____

_____

_____

2. In which ways can you economize on your marketing communication, using different printing, paper, format, etc.?

_____

_____

_____

_____

Day 10—Summary

- Your advantages need to be communicated in a convincing and compelling way.

- Messages in your marketing communication need to be articulated well and stated often.

- Advertising is just a subset of marketing communications.

- Communication is the key factor in determining whether you retain a customer, whether the customer spends more with you, and whether you outsell the competition.

- Clarity is just one of the primary considerations when developing your materials.

- Other considerations for marketing materials are focus, message, design, and credibility.

- Marketing materials are best used to inform, educate, and sell those who have already expressed an interest in your product or service.

- The creative plan directs the marketing communication.

- You should have a creative strategy for each component of your marketing communications plan.

- One goal of your creative idea is to get attention.

- State your benefit in such a way that will be accepted beyond doubt.

- Target prospects and customers need to be told what to do. Motivate for action.

- Don't let creativity overshadow the job of selling and marketing.

Aha! Moments:

Next-Level Springboards, Notes, To-Do's, etc.

Sanity Check

❏ Is this too much or not enough activity?

❏ Am I comfortable with the processes described here, the workload, and the implementation?

❏ Will the expected outcomes take me to a new level?

Additional Notes

DAY 11

Sunday	Monday	Tuesday	Wednesday	Thursday	Friday	Saturday
	1	2	3	4	5	6
7	8	9	10	11 ✔	12	13
14	15	16	17	18	19	20
21	22	23	24	25	26	27
28	29	30				

Advertising and Media Plan

MENTION "ADVERTISING" AND THE first thought that comes to mind for many is the plethora of television commercials we're all exposed to. Others think of the lineup of billboards along an interstate highway, the glossy slicks of magazines at the local newsstands, and the jingle-laden commercials heard on the radio.

These are all advertising methods most often used by traditional mass marketers. Advertising in the spirit of guerrilla marketing may or may not include these.

> Guerrillas use advertising that is more focused on a target market, less on the masses, and more personal, resulting in more sales conversions.

Advertising is the most visible form of marketing. It is also often referred to as the most elusive, seductive, and expensive branch of the marketing tree. Unfortunately, it is also the one that many businesses misunderstand the most. It is just one of the many guerrilla marketing weapons.

Media exposure and advertising can build a business—but if it's not planned right and executed correctly, it will eat up a marketing budget faster than you can say, "mass market." However, there is a right way to use this weapon.

Ad Development Exercise

Use the three-step creative formula from Day 10 to develop your ad.

1. What is the purpose of your ad?

_____

_____

_____

_____

2. What primary message do you want your advertising to convey? (Make sure to communicate benefits.)

_____

_____

_____

_____

3. What will be the look and feel of your ad?

_____

_____

_____

_____

Advertising Planner

Identify places to position your advertising, based on what your target market prospects see and hear and where they go when they need your product or service.

1. _____

2. _____

3. _____

4. _____

5. _____

For each potential vehicle for advertising, find out the following:

- The circulation or "reach" of the publication or broadcast

_____

_____

_____

- The geography of its coverage

_____

_____

_____

- Its target market

_____

_____

_____

- Its advertising rates

_____

_____

_____

- The frequency of distribution and/or publication to the target market

_____

_____

_____

What is your breakeven analysis if of you have to run a series of ads? (See scenarios below.)

_____

_____

Advertising Calculator: What Makes Sense (Cents!)

Breakeven Analysis

Fill in the blanks:

If I spend $_____ on my advertising campaign (the cost of six, 12, 24, or 27 ads), I will need $_____ to cover the cost of the campaign and to break even (before considering the "lifetime value" of the client). (The numbers in the above two blanks will be the same.)

$_____ is equal to the quantity of products or services sold (_____) times the unit price $(_____) of the number of products or services sold.

Identify quantity and products or services to arrive at the total revenue needed to break even.

Guerrilla Note: Lifetime Value of a Client

The lifetime value of a client value is the total benefit (tangible and intangible) that you receive from a client throughout the life of the relationship. Knowing this value will give you the proper perspective to predict or justify the impact of your management decisions, marketing decisions, and financial decisions. It is not a client evaluation based on one order, one sale, or one event. If a client orders today, there is a good chance he or she will order again.

For example, if you are selling consulting services and a client works with you for 12 months at a rate of $4,000 per month, then the current lifetime direct transaction value of that client is $4,000 x 12 months = $48,000.

It doesn't stop here. If that client refers another person to you who becomes a client and pays you for the same offering of services, you realize another $48,000 in client value.

Advertising Mock-up

Using the information from the exercise above, sketch out a thumbnail ad, complete with text and graphic concepts.

Note: Concentrate on the message here and just note any graphic design implication. When you get time to develop your ad and purchase your space or time, hire a professional designer to create the final version.

"Ad—ing" It All Up

Based on the above planning information, list the types of ads and sizes planned for the plan year.

_____

_____

_____

_____

_____

_____

Day 11—Summary

- Guerrillas use advertising that is more focused on a target market, less on the masses, and more personal, resulting in more sales conversions.

- Advertising is the most visible form of marketing. It is also often referred to as the most elusive, seductive, and expensive branch of the marketing tree.

- Advertising should not be intimidating.

- The most common form of advertising used by small businesses is advertising in newspapers and magazines.

- Advertising works best and feels best when it is balanced with all other marketing.

- Guerrillas use advertising to build share of mind.

- Advertising is a set of clear, creative messages with a guerrilla marketing budget of time, energy, and imagination.

- Pick the most frequent advertising vehicle that fits your budget and that hits your target market.

Aha! Moments:

Next-Level Springboards, Notes, To-Do's, etc.

Sanity Check

❏ Is this too much or not enough activity?

❏ Am I comfortable with the processes described here, the workload, and the implementation?

❏ Will the expected outcomes take me to a new level?

DAY 12

Sunday	Monday	Tuesday	Wednesday	Thursday	Friday	Saturday
	1	2	3	4	5	6
7	8	9	10	11	12 ✔	13
14	15	16	17	18	19	20
21	22	23	24	25	26	27
28	29	30				

Business Networking

WHEN IT COMES TO LOW- AND NO-COST marketing, networking ranks right at the top of the list. Harvey Mackay, author of *Dig Your Well Before You're Thirsty* (Currency/Doubleday Books, 1999) and *Swim with the Sharks Without Being Eaten Alive* (Ballantine Books, 1988), advises networking for anything: customers, contacts, prospects, referrals, jobs, material items, ideas, etc. In guerrilla marketing we use networking to make contact and establish relationships that eventually lead to increased business. This means networking for prospects who will eventually buy or refer those who will buy.

Networking is a planned process.

On Day 12 in *Guerrilla Marketing in 30 Days*, you learned that in order to network correctly and efficiently you have to follow a process. That process begins with selecting the right networking events to attend. You can't attend them all and all events are not the right ones for you to attend. It depends first on your business goals and second on your networking goals. These two exercises will start you off on the right foot.

Planning Your Events

Not every event where there are people to meet is the right networking event for you. Networking takes a plan. The plan is developed for efficiency and to leverage and manage time. Strategically choosing networking events ensures that you do so.

Networking Event Planner

EVENT	
Types of attendees (decision makers, purchasers, business owners, etc.)	
Probability of meeting the right prospect	
Is this networking event the best use of my time?	
Primary networking goal at this event	
Does the event have a clear agenda?	
Do I know anyone else attending the event?	
How many people are estimated to attend?	
Was the event promoted to my target market?	
What is the sponsoring organization?	

After going through this exercise, you are in a position to prioritize which events are right for you and which would be the best use of your time. From this you can then allocate your total time and establish how many networking events you will attend in a month's time.

How many events will you attend this month? _____

List the types and exact names of the events you will attend in the coming year, based on the above planner information.

_____

_____

_____

_____

_____

Exercise: Setting Networking Goals

Showing up at a networking event without networking goals almost guarantees that the event will be social for you. Knowing whether this is the right event for you depends on whether it is likely that you will be able to meet your networking goals.

1. How many business cards do I want to receive? _____

2. How many business cards will I note something of interest on, for follow-up? _____

3. What titles of people do I want to meet? _____

4, Are there one or two specific people at an event that I want to meet? _____

5. Will there be a mutual acquaintance attending the event who can introduce me to the person or people I want to meet? _____

6. How will I communicate the fact that I want to follow up with someone subsequent to the event (similar to a close in sales)? _____

7. With how many people from this event do I realistically want to start and maintain a relationship? _____

Whom Should I Target with My Networking?

How do you know whom to contact? How do you know you won't be wasting your time with a particular person or, more specifically, that you will achieve your networking goals?

The real answer is that you don't always know. Businesses that have the same types of prospects as you and have the same common interests are usually good for making contacts. Businesses that complement your products and services are good networking targets. An estate planning attorney complements a life insurance sales representative. A graphic designer complements a printing company. A photographer complements a wedding planner or caterer.

People who could best assist you with referrals and building relationships in similar industries are your best networking targets. The mindset here is networking for the indirect referrals. Very little "actual business" is done at a networking event. Most true business starts in the follow-up phase, when relationships are initiated and eventually nurtured.

Targeting Formula

1. What types of companies have the same types as prospects as mine?

_____

_____

_____

_____

2. What types of companies and organizations have the same interests as mine?

_____

_____

_____

_____

Networking Factoid

Power Partner: A company that has similar goals, similar values, similar prospects and target markets, and similar deliveries to market, e.g., a realtor and a mortgage broker.

3. What types of companies would make good Power Partners?

_____

_____

_____

4. Who are potential Power Partners?

_____

_____

_____

_____

5. Who can assist me with referrals?

_____

_____

_____

_____

6. What specific companies will we work with as Power Partners?

_____

_____

_____

_____

Relationship Building in Networking

People like to do business with those they like and trust. This can be done even at a price premium. Can this trust and confidence be established at one networking event with one introduction? No, it can't. It takes follow-up, getting to know each other, finding common ground, interests, and compatibility.

Part of relationship building, especially at the start, is being interested in the other person—his or her business, family, hobbies, goals and aspirations, etc.—and showing that interest.

In addition to interest, an integral part of networking and relationship building is listening. Hearing what the other person has to say is more important than delivering your sales pitch instantly. Many times while listening you can pick up signals about business potential, direct and indirect.

In the spirit of guerrilla marketing, business is not always measured by the number of orders. Many times a good measure of a successful business is the number of relationships.

Relationship-Building Test

Before the Event

1. What listening skills will I try to excel at?

_____

_____

2. What problems that a prospect states are signals of business potential for me?

_____

_____

After the Event

1. Did a prospect state a challenge about himself or herself or someone else?

_____

_____

2. How can I get to the "someone else" to solve that problem?

_____

_____

3. How many relationships a month can I realistically develop?

_____

_____

Follow-Up

The key to lead success is follow-up. Just like any other form of marketing, it sometimes takes a number of times before a lead can be converted to interest and from there to eventual closing of the sale.

Follow up on each new contact and invite him or her to coffee, lunch, or an after-hours meeting. Send a card or a note to those of interest immediately. Follow up and schedule a true business meeting.

Contact and follow up with information that may be of use or of interest to your contact. This can start and build a great relationship.

Follow-up Motivator

1. What can I do for the next year to continue the relationship? How will I keep in touch?

_____

_____

_____

_____

2. What follow-up things can I do for the first step of follow-up?

_____

_____

_____

_____

3. How soon after the event will I start the follow-up process?

_____

_____

_____

_____

4. What will the contact and I discuss at a follow-up meeting?

_____

_____

_____

_____

5. What outcomes do I want from a follow-up meeting?

_____

_____

_____

_____

Post-Event Checklist

❑ Did I have goals before arriving?

❑ Did I arrive early?

❑ Did I stay late?

❑ Did I get a chance to review the list of participants?

❑ Did I help at the registration desk?

❑ Did I target a few potential Power Partners?

❑ Did I listen well?

❑ Did I maintain good eye contact?

❑ Did I show more interest in my contacts than myself?

❑ Was I enthusiastic?

❑ Did I ask enough questions but not too many?

❑ Did I gather information as a result of my conversation and questions?

❑ Did that include personal information of note?

❑ Do I know what problems and challenges the people I met need help with?

1. Who did I pass out business cards to?

_____   _____

_____   _____

_____   _____

_____   _____

_____   _____

2. Who did I receive business cards from?

_____   _____

_____   _____

_____   _____

_____   _____

3. Who was at the event that I wanted to meet but I didn't get a chance?

_____   _____

_____   _____

_____   _____

_____   _____

_____   _____

4. How can I meet them now?
   ❏ Another networking event
   ❏ Mutual friend
   ❏ A follow-up note
   ❏ A phone call
   ❏ An e-mail
   ❏ A visit

Day 12—Summary

- The act of working, communicating, and interacting with groups is what is known as networking.

- Networking should be an integral part of any guerrilla marketing plan.

- Networking is contact to establish relationships that can lead to business.

- Your goal of attending a networking event is to meet people with whom to follow up and start a relationship.

- Not every event where people meet is always the right event to network.

- Choose networking events that allow you to meet your networking goals.

- The goal of networking is to make contacts and get information that leads to relationships that lead to increased business.

- People who could best assist you with referrals and building relationships in similar industries are your best networking targets.

- A good measure of a successful business is the number of relationships.

- The key to lead success is follow-up.

Aha! Moments:

Next-Level Springboards, Notes, To-Do's, etc.

Sanity Check

- ❏ Is this too much or not enough activity?
- ❏ Am I comfortable with the processes described here, the workload, and the implementation?
- ❏ Will the expected outcomes take me to a new level?

DAY 13

Sunday	Monday	Tuesday	Wednesday	Thursday	Friday	Saturday
	1	2	3	4	5	6
7	8	9	10	11	12	13 ✔
14	15	16	17	18	19	20
21	22	23	24	25	26	27
28	29	30				

Strategic Alliances and Fusion Marketing

THE OFFICIAL WEBSTER'S DICTIONARY definition of *strategic alliance* fits, even as it relates to guerrilla marketing: a merging of diverse, distinct, or separate elements into a unified whole. Doing this under the guise of a business partnership is *fusion marketing*.

Business connections with other businesses that are not customers are often referred to as *strategic alliances*, *affinity marketing*, *joint venturing*, *affiliate relationships*, or *fusion marketing*. In guerrilla language, we use the term *fusion marketing*. Fusion marketing is combining the efforts of two entities to "explode" their joint marketing efforts.

> Fusion marketing is nothing more than a strategic alliance with another business.

Fusion marketing makes sense when two companies have similar target markets, similar prospects, and similar values. Take, for example, the whole world of online marketing, a common area for fusion marketing. Here, companies work together to display one another's information. It can be as simple as a link to each other's site or links to articles, order forms, application, case studies, etc. Each participant gains more exposure while adding to the content and quality of each other's marketing.

Power Partner Selection

1. What types of companies would be good Power Partners for you?

_____

_____

_____

_____

_____

2. Of the companies listed above, which ones have prospects similar to your prospects?

_____

_____

_____

_____

_____

3. Which of these companies have similar business values and goals and a similar marketing attitude and mindset and would be willing to share with you, i.e., would be good Power Partners for you and your business?

_____

_____

_____

_____

_____

Fusion Marketing Sharing

1. What could you offer a fusion marketing partner?

   Web site link   Y ❑ N ❑

   Article to post online or hand out Y ❑ N ❑

   Sign or display exchange Y ❑ N ❑

   Coupon exchange   Y ❑ N ❑

   Brochure or flier exchange Y ❑ N ❑

   Other _____ Y ❑ N ❑

Fusion Marketing Action Plan

1. With your chosen Power Partner, discuss and brainstorm additional marketing ideas, especially those related to online marketing.

   _____

   _____

   _____

   _____

   _____

2. Which idea can be put to a test for both partners and what would the test consist of?

   _____

   _____

   _____

   _____

   _____

3. How will the test be measured and what will the follow-up date be?

   _____

   _____

   _____

   _____

   _____

Fusion Marketing Funding

1. Who would benefit by sponsoring something that you do, e.g., a seminar, a Web site page, another type of event, a contribution to a non-profit organization, etc.?

_____

_____

_____

_____

_____

2. Which suppliers have cooperative advertising funds available?

_____

_____

_____

_____

_____

3. Ask the suppliers without co-op funds about the possibilities of creating a program.

_____

_____

_____

_____

Day 13—Summary

- Fusion marketing is nothing more than a strategic alliance with another business.

- Fusion marketing makes sense when two companies have similar target markets and similar values.

- Fusion marketing is one of the most underused, inexpensive, effective methods of guerrilla marketing.

- Guerrillas align themselves with a wide assortment of fusion marketing partners.

- Two forms of fusion marketing that aren't necessarily labeled as such are co-op advertising funds and sponsorships.

- Affiliate marketing programs are simple partnerships between a seller and another seller or a distributor when both want to reach beyond selling their own products and services. Affiliate marketing is another form of fusion marketing.

- Two marketers are better than one, especially if the two share one cost.

Aha! Moments:

Next-Level Springboards, Notes, To-Do's, etc.

Sanity Check

❏ Is this too much or not enough activity?

❏ Am I comfortable with the processes described here, the workload, and the implementation?

❏ Will the expected outcomes take me to a new level?

Additional Notes

DAY 14

Sunday	Monday	Tuesday	Wednesday	Thursday	Friday	Saturday
	1	2	3	4	5	6
7	8	9	10	11	12	13
14 ✔	15	16	17	18	19	20
21	22	23	24	25	26	27
28	29	30				

Direct Selling

WHEN THINKING OF HOW BEST TO GET your marketing message to a prospect, face to face always wins out. One-on-one interaction allows for dialogue. A postcard can't answer a question on the spot. A radio commercial can't overcome an objection by a prospect. A sign can't supply additional information when a prospect requests it. Personal selling can do all these things.

When the early caveman was selling his wheel and people asked questions, he could answer. When asked, "What is that round thing that you are selling used for?" he could demonstrate. He could collect cave bucks once he answered, once he sold.

Selling has often been called the distribution arm of marketing.

Personal selling, whether you are a caveman or a guerrilla, allows you to develop and adjust a message to satisfy a prospect's need for information or to answer a question. Developing and adjusting messages is marketing. Satisfying prospects' needs is guerrilla marketing.

Dialogue happens when you are face to face with a prospect. Personal selling is dialogue between you and your prospect with the objective of getting the prospect to give you money in exchange for your products and services, whether that money is cave bucks or contemporary legal tender.

Your Selling Process

1. Before working through this workbook Day, describe your selling process.

_____

_____

_____

_____

2. Do you have listening as part of your process? Y ☐ N ☐

3. Do you have sales goals? Y ☐ N ☐
   If yes, outline them here:

_____

_____

_____

_____

_____

4. How many prospects do you call a day?

_____

5. How many appointments do you get from those calls?

_____

6. How many sales do you get from those appointments?

_____

7. What level of sales do you need a month for your company to be profitable?

_____

8. How many salespeople do you have?

_____

9. How often will you call on a prospect or customer?
   Before you stop trying to get them to buy

_____

After the initial sale is made.

_____

Understand the numbers above and how they work for you and your business. Then, set selling goals accordingly.

_____

_____

_____

_____

_____

The Sales Presentation: The Actual Sales Call

1. What question will you ask your prospect to understand their ...

   Interest?

   _____

   _____

   Challenges?

   _____

   _____

   Objections?

   _____

   _____

   Likelihood of buying?

   _____

   _____

2. What uses of your product or service can you demonstrate for a prospect?

   _____

   _____

   _____

3. List 25 points of your sales presentation.

_____   _____
_____   _____
_____   _____
_____   _____
_____   _____
_____   _____
_____   _____
_____   _____
_____   _____
_____   _____
_____   _____
_____   _____
_____

4. Now condense your 25 points to the five most important.

_____
_____
_____
_____
_____

Reversing Roles

1. When was the last time you were on the purchasing side of a sales presentation?

_____

2. What do you remember about this?

_____

_____

_____

_____

_____

3. What was good about it?

_____

_____

_____

4. What did you not like about it?

_____

_____

_____

5. Did you buy? Y ❑ N ❑

6. Why or why not?

_____

_____

_____

7. Adapt your sales process/plan accordingly.

_____

_____

_____

The Objection Objector

1. List all the potential objections that a prospect will make when "being sold to."

_____

_____

_____

_____

_____

_____

_____

_____

_____

2. Now write out the script for the ways to overcome each of these objections.

_____

_____

_____

_____

_____

_____

_____

_____

_____

_____

_____

Day 14—Summary

- Selling has often been called the distribution arm of marketing.

- Personal selling allows you to develop and adjust a message to satisfy a prospect's need for information or to answer a question.

- Nothing develops a personal relationship better than personal contact. Direct selling is personal contact.

- Preparation is part of personal selling.

- Business will be transacted when the prospect decides that you can solve his or her problems or enhance his or her business, quality of work life, or profits.

- Identifying the next mutually agreed upon action is a close.

- Understanding what a prospect wants and needs and hearing it directly tells you what to target, what to sell, and what problems to solve.

- Selling is a very important part of the marketing process, but it is not a replacement for it.

- Figuring out how to win a customer's time, consideration, and money is the key to successful selling.

- Marketing cannot exist without sales and sales cannot exist without marketing.

Aha! Moments:

Next-Level Springboards, Notes, To-Do's, etc.

Sanity Check

❏ Is this too much or not enough activity?

❏ Am I comfortable with the processes described here, the workload, and the implementation?

❏ Will the expected outcomes take me to a new level?

Additional Notes

Sunday	Monday	Tuesday	Wednesday	Thursday	Friday	Saturday
	1	2	3	4	5	6
7	8	9	10	11	12	13
14	15 ✔	16	17	18	19	20
21	22	23	24	25	26	27
28	29	30				

Telephone Selling and Marketing

TO TAKE FULL ADVANTAGE OF GUERRILLA marketing credos of time efficiency, optimum energy expended, and creativity and imagination to the max, marketing and selling need to take place when you're not present in person with the prospect or customer.

Tele-selling, telemarketing, or selling and marketing by phone: all happen without you being physically present with the prospect or customer. Sometimes people buy over the phone and sometimes they don't. Be prepared for the average of this weapon. Measure the number of calls, the time involved, and the resulting sales and profits. If the profits are there and are worth the number of calls made, then selling by telephone is a worthwhile weapon in your arsenal. If you are making too many calls without enough results, either revise your approach or put this weapon in the guerrilla recycle bin.

> Telephone sales are one of the fastest-growing segments of the sales profession.

Our "territories" are expanding minute by minute, with some even going global. With the way travel costs are rising and the amount of time salespeople travel, the cost of sales is escalating. On Day 14 you were cautioned about the one disadvantage of personal selling being high costs. It is almost becoming a world of travelers selling instead of sellers traveling. Selling by telephone overcomes some of these high costs of true selling.

Direct Selling/Direct Telephone Selling

Review the action steps from Day 14, Direct Selling, and see which ones adapt directly to selling with the telephone.

_____

_____

_____

_____

_____

_____

_____

_____

_____

_____

_____

_____

_____

_____

_____

_____

_____

_____

_____

_____

_____

_____

_____

Ready, Set, Ring ...

Write down your best "opening statement" for your tele-selling phone call. This will vary with different products and services and different emphases. It may also change depending on the customer or prospect and your relationship.

_____

_____

_____

_____

_____

_____

_____

_____

_____

Script out your offering of value for prospects.

For example: "My name is _____ with _____. We specialize in _____ for _____. Could this solve any of your current challenges?"

_____

_____

_____

_____

_____

_____

_____

_____

_____

_____

_____

_____

_____

Script out your statement for a follow-up call.

For example: "Hi, this is _____. On _____ we spoke about _____. I'm calling to see if _____."

_____

_____

_____

_____

_____

_____

_____

_____

Telephone the numbers on your list to confirm the name, the pronunciation of that name, and the position of decision makers. Script out what you will say on this call.

For example: "I need to send information to _____ Can you verify the spelling of their name and the address and position?" If you have only the title, use it to get the name.

For example: " … and what is the name of your purchasing agent?" Keep track of your calls and the resulting information here and in a separate log.

_____

_____

_____

_____

_____

_____

_____

_____

Suggestion: If your list is in alphabetical order, start in the middle or the end of the list, not the beginning.

Based on the above information, our telemarketing sales goals are:

_____

_____

_____

_____

_____

Day 15—Summary

- Selling and marketing by phone happen without you being physically present with the prospect or customer.

- Selling by telephone overcomes some of the high costs of selling.

- Some of your customers don't want to wait for you or your salesperson to visit. That's where tele-selling comes in.

- Your tele-presence or identity is the combination of all the tele-related marketing weapons in your arsenal.

- Tele-selling closes the business when you can't be there.

- "Good phone" uncovers a prospect's need and wants and then offers convincing reasons to buy from you.

- Presenting on the telephone is quick and effective communication that you have something of value for the prospect as soon as you have learned more about him or her.

- Telephone communication is used to build and maintain relationships.

- Prospects want phone calls that focus on them.

- Having the right message, reaching the right target, and responding with the right question or presentation will determine the outcome of a tele-selling effort.

Aha! Moments:

Next-Level Springboards, Notes, To-Do's, etc.

Sanity Check

❏ Is this too much or not enough activity?

❏ Am I comfortable with the processes described here, the workload, and the implementation?

❏ Will the expected outcomes take me to a new level?

DAY 16

Sunday	Monday	Tuesday	Wednesday	Thursday	Friday	Saturday
	1	2	3	4	5	6
7	8	9	10	11	12	13
14	15	16 ✔	17	18	19	20
21	22	23	24	25	26	27
28	29	30				

Printed Collateral, Brochures, and Sales Sheets

COLLATERAL IS SOMETIMES CALLED SALES collateral, marketing collateral, print collateral, or just collateral. When used in this sense, it is supporting sales, supporting marketing, and supporting guerrilla efforts.

> Sales collateral is as much a part of the
> marketing process as a salesperson.

When considering all the print collateral options, you only have to go as far as looking at your overall marketing plan developed on Day 7. In that plan you discuss:

- Communicating the benefits of your products and services to the marketplace
- Keeping in touch with clients about your company, people, products, services, and special offers
- Packaging
- Your identity
- New product development and introductions
- Your selling process and presentation

119

- Awareness and PR campaigns
- Information, persuading, and answering questions about anything to do with your company or organization

If these are in your plan from Day 7, then you have a great starting point for developing your print collateral. Each one of these takes one or more print collateral pieces. If they are not in your plan, revisit and revise accordingly.

Direct Mail Collateral Audit

1. Which pieces of mail in the past few days or weeks have you thrown away?

_____

_____

_____

_____

2. Why did you throw them away? Jot down the reasons: e.g., wasn't interested in product, didn't need it, didn't like it, looked like a shoddy offering, etc.

_____

_____

_____

_____

3. Which pieces of mail in the past few days or weeks have you kept?

_____

_____

_____

_____

4. Why did you keep those pieces of mail? Jot down the reasons: e.g., was interested in the product or service, noticed something I needed, noticed something I wanted, looked like a great offer, grabbed my attention with something, etc.

_____

_____

_____

_____

Adapting What Works, Creating the Rest

1. What three companies' brochures have you noticed, liked, and kept?

_____

_____

_____

_____

2. Looking at the direct mail pieces that you liked and kept and the brochures that you liked and kept, which components of them can you use or adapt in your collateral marketing?

_____

_____

_____

_____

3. What other headlines, pictures, bullet points, FAQs, or other information of your own can you add to the above components and ideas for your collateral pieces?

_____

_____

_____

_____

Collateral Planning

1. What is your objective for other print collateral?

_____

_____

_____

_____

2. How will you use the various pieces of your marketing collateral?

_____

_____

_____

_____

3. How will you get the collateral to your prospects?

_____

_____

_____

_____

4. What costs are involved with each piece of collateral?

_____

_____

_____

_____

5. What budget do you need to produce a brochure that looks professional, does the right job, is timeless, and is appealing to your prospects?

_____

_____

_____

_____

6. Can you afford this budget?   Yes ❑ Maybe ❑ Not Yet ❑ No ❑

7. What identity items do you want included in your collateral?

_____

_____

_____

_____

8. How many different ways can you use each individual collateral piece?

	Collateral Piece 1	Collateral Piece 2	Collateral Piece 3
Direct Mail Piece	_____	_____	_____
Posted on Web Site	_____	_____	_____
Handout Flier	_____	_____	_____
Enclosed in Packaging	_____	_____	_____
Other	_____	_____	_____

Casual Collateral Observation

1. What other printed marketing have you noticed?

_____

_____

2. Where did you see it?

_____

_____

3. What made you notice it?

_____

_____

4. Did the collateral influence your purchase decision? Yes ❑ No ❑

5. Based on the above information, your planned collateral pieces in summary for the plan year will consist of the following:

_____

_____

_____

_____

_____

Day 16—Summary

- Collateral is sometimes called *sales collateral*, *marketing collateral*, *print collateral*, or *just collateral*. It supports both sales and marketing.

- Collateral offers the reader a unique brand experience to hold, to touch, to feel, to fold, and to reread, connecting the reader with the printed piece and leaving a lasting impression that starts a relationship.

- Good print collateral contains information your customers and prospects need to make purchase decisions.

- Print collateral is your "in absentia" sales force.

- One key to collateral is providing information that will induce the prospect to purchase or providing information that will answer questions leading to a purchase.

- The best collateral format to reach your target market is brochures, fliers, circulars, business cards, fact sheets, and other print materials, all carrying your identity, reputation, and information into the marketplace.

- One of the main pieces of your company's collateral collection is a brochure.

- Another popular form of collateral is the sales sheet; sometimes referred to as a *one sheet*, a *fact sheet*, a *sales flier*, a *spec sheet*, or a *product data sheet*.

- The key to collateral is to plan out the pieces, plan the budget accordingly, be consistent with their use, and use them as support vehicles.

Aha! Moments:

Next-Level Springboards, Notes, To-Do's, etc.

Sanity Check

❏ Is this too much or not enough activity?

❏ Am I comfortable with the processes described here, the workload, and the implementation?

❏ Will the expected outcomes take me to a new level?

DAY 17

Sunday	Monday	Tuesday	Wednesday	Thursday	Friday	Saturday
	1	2	3	4	5	6
7	8	9	10	11	12	13
14	15	16	17 ✔	18	19	20
21	22	23	24	25	26	27
28	29	30				

Direct Mail

WHY IS *DIRECT MAIL* CALLED DIRECT MAIL? Why isn't it called "indirect mail" or just "mail"? Direct mail is simply direct communication to targeted prospects and customers. This form of one-to-one marketing is the opposite of mass marketing.

Other forms of marketing and advertising communicate to the masses. With mass communication, you're never really sure who is receiving your message. With direct mail, you communicate one on one directly to your intended audience. It is more of a rifle shot to your target market, a direct rifle shot. You control who receives your message, how often they see it, and how many are reached: all direct effects of direct mail.

> Direct mail is one of the most efficient and cost-effective ways to get a message to your target.

Direct mail is one of the most efficient and cost-effective ways to get a message to a target audience. This coupled with the fact that one of your top priorities as a guerrilla business is reaching your target audience makes direct mail the marketing medium of choice for you and many other guerrilla marketers. Direct mail informs, persuades, and educates prospects who are inaccessible by other means. Direct mail helps to level the playing field for small companies going against larger companies. The fight is for the mindshare of one targeted person.

In the spirit of guerrilla marketing, these factors translate into one of the more profitable ways to touch existing and potential clients. It also translates into an effective way to get your prospects to open their wallets.

Direct Mail Calculator: What Makes Sense

Breakeven Analysis

Fill in the blanks:

If I spend $_____ on my direct mail campaign, I will need $_____ to cover the cost of the campaign and to break even (before considering the "lifetime value" of the client).

(The numbers in the above two blanks will be the same.)

$_____ is equal to the quantity of products or services sold _____ times the unit price $_____ of the number of products or services sold.

Identify quantity and products or services to arrive at the total revenue needed to break even.

Choosing Your Preferred Outside Vendors

When looking at all of the components of a direct mail campaign, it quickly becomes clear that you probably can't do it alone. Very seldom are businesses equipped, set up, or in possession of the expertise to design, print, process, sort, and deliver direct mail. Relying on preferred outside vendors to carry these operations out is essential to the success of a direct mail campaign and the proper use of your time, energy, and expertise.

Service/Product	Contact Information	Details of Contact/Follow-Up
Design/Writing	_____	_____
Printing	_____	_____
Mail Prep/Processing	_____	_____
Other		
Delivery	_____	_____
Converting	_____	_____
Staging	_____	_____
Inventory	_____	_____
Other	_____	_____

Direct Mail Target Planner

Understanding the answers to the questions and components in this workbook will provide you the information to "drill down" and refine your target market with the greatest of precision. The more complete your answers and thoughts are, the more precise your target market will be. The more precise your target definition is, the higher the response rate you can expect from your marketing campaigns. These worksheets are not only to define your target market but also to drill down and refine as precisely as possible the people you will target with your marketing. In direct mail and any other direct marketing, precision wins out.

Target Market Worksheet

1. What do I sell?

_____

_____

2. What are the three top benefits that I offer?

_____

_____

_____

3. What am I really selling?

_____

_____

4. Who typically buys this product or service?

_____

_____

5. *For business to business marketing:*

   ■ What industries are likely prospects for my products or services?

_____

_____

   ■ What are the primary SIC or NAICS codes of targeted businesses?

_____

_____

- What are the secondary, related SIC or NAICS codes of targeted businesses?

_____

_____

- What size are the companies?

  Sales dollars _____

  Number of employees _____

- Location/geography

_____

- Years in business

_____

- Who in the companies buys the products or services?

  ❏ C-Level officers

  ❏ Purchasing manager

  ❏ Department head/supervisor

  ❏ Actual user

- Trade associations that the companies might belong to

_____

- Publications of the trade

_____

_____

- Identity—conservative or flashy? prominent or well known? established or start-up? community-oriented or national in scope?

_____

_____

For marketing to consumers:

- Age group that the product or service is designed for:

_____

- Who uses the product/service?

_____

_____

- Where is the product/service purchased?

_____

_____

- Demographics of consumers:

  Income levels: _____

  Geographic location: _____

  Marital status: _____

  Children: _____

  Education level: _____

  Home ownership: _____

  Publications read: _____

This checklist will take you right up to the point of campaign execution

❏ Decide on a tentative target market

_____

_____

❏ Find catalogs, magazines, reports that serve your target market.

_____

_____

❏ Search out the publications' list managers.

_____

_____

❏ Inquire about purchasing or renting a list of subscribers.

_____

_____

❏ Investigate conditions for use.

❏ If no list is available directly, contact a list broker.

❏ Define list specifications with a list broker.

❏ Obtain a count for list members fitting this specification.

❏ Run costs on the count, selects, and overlays

❏ Establish total campaign costs using this cost component and take to the next step of the campaign.

Direct Mail Message Planner

One of the four primary components of direct marketing is the marketing message. Essentially this is the component that defines what you will say and how you will say it to your targeted prospect. Answer the following questions in detail.

1. Do you have a strong and clear offer?

_____

_____

2. Is your offer clearly something of value?

_____

_____

3. What is the best offer you can use?

_____

_____

4. Is your headline big, bold, and attention-getting?

_____

_____

5. Does your first paragraph pull the reader into your copy?

_____

_____

6. Are benefits pointed out and emphasized?

_____

_____

7. Do you state the challenges and suggest that there is a solution available?

_____

_____

8. Are your paragraphs short and readable?

_____

_____

9. Does the copy flow logically from point to point?

_____

_____

10. Is your language understandable without assuming too much knowledge on the part of your readers?

_____

_____

11. Have you included the high-impact words and emotional appeals?

_____

_____

12. Is your copy written as if you were having a conversation one on one?

_____

_____

13. Do you have a call to action that will generate a response?

_____

_____

14. What is that call to action?

_____

_____

15. Is it clear what action you want your prospect to take?

_____

_____

16. Do you make it easy for your prospect to respond?

_____

_____

17. Do you have a deadline for a response or some other sense of urgency copy?

_____

_____

18. If you're using a letter, do you have a hard-hitting P.S. restating benefits and some value?

_____

_____

Direct Mail Frequency Planner

Whether you are considering direct marketing online or offline, it takes repetition and consistency to achieve your marketing goals. You must get people to notice your message, to read it, to absorb it, and to understand it enough to feel motivated to take action. Because of natural probability, some people will respond immediately, on the first message, to a direct marketing offer. Others will need to see the message more than once, and probably many more times, before responding to an offer.

Direct marketing and direct sales studies have shown that the highest probability for a sale occurs during the follow-up process. That might sound like common sense, but it is not common practice. This follow-up process must be done right, with consistency, in order to be effective. Jim Rohn, the famed personal development motivator, states that "without a sense of urgency, desire loses its value." Correspondingly, without consistent follow-up and attention, prospects and customers lose desire. Collection agencies and debt collectors prove this every day with their collection letters and warnings.

Timing and Frequency Checklist

1. What is the planned send date?

_____

2. Is there a time of day to consider for delivery, if it can be executed?

_____

3. What day do you want the mail to hit: consideration of delivery time—instantaneous if e-mail, longer if first-class or bulk mail?

_____

4. How frequently will you mail the pieces of this campaign?

_____

5. Will the same piece/message or different pieces/messages be sent during this one campaign?

_____

6. What holidays and any seasonal months or weeks should be avoided?

_____

_____

7. What particular deadlines and senses of urgency need to be considered?

_____

_____

8. Are there any related events to tie into?

_____

_____

9. Based on the above information, what will be your planned frequency for mailings?

_____

_____

Direct Mail Vehicle Planner

One of the four primary components of direct marketing is the marketing vehicle. Essentially, this is the component that defines how you will reach your targeted prospect.

1. Which is better for my target market-a letter, a postcard, or a three-dimensional package?

_____

_____

2. What is the design?

_____

_____

3. Are there design considerations that will affect the postage rate?

_____

_____

4. Is the design printer-friendly or will it cost a lot and take a lot of time to produce?

_____

_____

5. Based on the above planning information, the following campaigns are specifically planned with the associated objective of each campaign:

_____

_____

_____

_____

_____

_____

_____

_____

Day 17-Summary

- Direct mail is junk when it is of no interest to the receiver. Targeted to those with interest, this direct form of marketing is no longer junk.

- Direct mail is one of the most efficient and cost-effective ways to get a message to a target market.

- With direct mail, you control who receives your message.

- Direct mail uses a wide variety of marketing communication pieces.

- Direct mail is efficient and cost-effective because of the strengths and advantages associated with it:
  - Personalization
  - Targeted and focused
  - Call to action
  - Sales-oriented
  - Measurable

- Key components of direct mail: message, vehicle, target, and frequency.

- As long as the U.S. Postal Service is in existence, direct mail marketing will be strong.

Aha! Moments:

Next-Level Springboards, Notes, To-Do's, etc.

Sanity Check

❏ Is this too much or not enough activity?
❏ Am I comfortable with the processes described here, the workload, and the imple-mentation?
❏ Will the expected outcomes take me to a new level?

DAY 18

Sunday	Monday	Tuesday	Wednesday	Thursday	Friday	Saturday
	1	2	3	4	5	6
7	8	9	10	11	12	13
14	15	16	17	18 ✔	19	20
21	22	23	24	25	26	27
28	29	30				

Radio/Television/Cable TV

WITH TV SETS IN OVER 99 PERCENT of our homes and radios in 95 percent of cars, your target market is reachable by the airwaves. Venturing into this advertising arena can seem at first to be un-guerrilla like. By Day 18 you know enough about guerrilla marketing to realize that using these weapons in the right way, with the right plan, and with a profit orientation can be the difference between marginal results and success in your guerrilla marketing attack.

Not only do 90 percent of men, women, and teens listen to radio, but in our very mobile society, where consumers have less and less time for fixed-attention media, you can reach them all. People can hear your radio advertisement while driving, jogging, walking in the park, dining, or relaxing in their backyards.

> In our very mobile society, where consumers have less and less time for fixed-attention media, you can reach them all.

Here's the best way to think about radio. How can you sell, promote, brand, and continue to make targeted prospects aware of your product or service in 60 seconds? That's the standard length of a radio commercial slot. Crafting your marketing message to fit that slot is the challenge and opportunity of radio.

Mention "television" and immediately people think big company advertising. With the growth of cable and regional television advertising, a small business can benefit from television just like the big guys. Look how cable stations have popped up everywhere in recent few years. Tune into your satellite dish and the choices of cable television channels are virtually endless.

All these channels need advertising revenue to remain on the air. These stations are supported by advertising just like the network television stations. With the increase in television stations and the increased competition in this arena, cable television advertising has become a lot less expensive than traditional advertising. Many stations are offering very affordable rate packages, easily in reach for guerrilla marketers in small businesses and organizations.

TV is a perfect medium for introducing a new product or showing a comparison. It is a visual advertising medium. One good test of this is to see if you can tell what is being advertised with the sound turned down. The script is a support to the visuals. You have a good script if you can close your eyes and tell what product or service is being advertised. Using both audio and visual with this weapon of mass marketing, you will hit your target effectively.

Radio Listening Audit: What Do You Hear?

What type of radio programming do members of your target market listen to?

_____

_____

_____

Radio Ad Creative Development

Write a 15-second ad like Books-a-Go-Go for your product or service and your company.

_____

_____

_____

_____

_____

_____

_____

_____

_____

Mini Checklist:

Time it _____

Record it _____

Try different voice inflections _____

Expand your 15-second ad to 30 seconds. Let others hear it and see what they think of it.

_____

_____

_____

_____

_____

_____

_____

_____

_____

_____

_____

_____

"Seeing What You Hear"

Listen to the radio for the next five commercial advertisements. Visualize how you would tell each of these "ad stories" with visuals. Write out or draw roughly each theme or action moment block by block, kind of like newspaper comic strips. In the video business this is called storyboarding.

Now take your own marketing message, your radio or print ad, and do the same story-boarding exercise.

Your Television World

1. What are the TV viewing habits of your target audience?

_____

_____

_____

2. Are your competitors advertising on TV? If so, which ones and what is the main message, hook, and appearance of their ads?

_____

_____

_____

_____

_____

_____

Planning Your Airwaves

1. What message will you want to get across to your audience in your radio and TV advertising?

_____

_____

_____

2. What is the break-even volume you must attain to pay for the cost of your product sold and the airtime bought for radio? What is the break-even volume for TV?

_____

_____

_____

3. Can you afford to run a commercial for ...
   one month? _____
   three months? _____
   six months? _____

4. Based on the above planning information, the total on-air budget for each commercial is:

_____

_____

_____

5. The associated production budget for each commercial is:

_____

_____

_____

6. The planned frequency is as follows:
   Radio _____
   Television _____
   Cable TV _____

Day 18-Summary

- There are radio and TV alternatives and strategies that are very affordable for small businesses.

- The best way to think about radio is this: How can you sell, promote, brand, and continue to make targeted prospects aware of your product or service in 60 seconds?

- Repetition on the radio builds awareness.

- Radio is effective in combination with all of your other marketing; it represents another touch to the prospect with your message and your identity.

- TV advertising is nothing more than using the same headlines and the same marketing message as used in radio and adding graphics and visuals to it.

- Viewers will remember how they felt watching an ad more than every detail of the ad. You want viewers to feel good but also feel informed, persuaded, and motivated enough to buy your product or service.

- The key to TV advertising is also repetition.

- Products, services, and businesses gain instant credibility if they advertise on television.

- A television target audience will call you if you tell them what to do, what's in it for them, and how they can reach you easily.

- With the increase in television stations, cable television advertising has become a lot less expensive than traditional television advertising, making it affordable.

Aha! Moments:

Next-Level Springboards, Notes, To-Do's, etc.

Sanity Check

❏ Is this too much or not enough activity?

❏ Am I comfortable with the processes described here, the workload, and the implementation?

❏ Will the expected outcomes take me to a new level?

Sunday	Monday	Tuesday	Wednesday	Thursday	Friday	Saturday
	1	2	3	4	5	6
7	8	9	10	11	12	13
14	15	16	17	18	19 ✔	20
21	22	23	24	25	26	27
28	29	30				

Marketing Hooks

HOOKS ATTRACT ATTENTION TO YOU and your business. They are also used in your one-on-one interaction with others. In the world of networking, you are often asked to give your 30-second commercial about you and your company. How many 30-second commercials do you remember from networking events you have attended? Why don't you remember them? More importantly, why do you remember the few that you do? Whatever it is, something "hooked" you. You as a prospect bit the bait. You wanted to know more. You asked more questions. These reactions are all characteristics of a good marketing hook.

> A memorable hook attracts attention to your marketing message, what you are saying, and what your business is all about.

Hooks also come in the form of jingles, taglines, and memorable ad content. If you remembered one of these from a company or advertiser, you were hooked. If you told someone about one of these, you were hooked.

A marketing hook is a start. It holds your bait. It's a taste of more to come. "Leave them begging for more" was never truer than it is with a marketing hook. The best part is the cost. A marketing hook costs you nothing. This is guerrilla marketing, isn't it? Imagination is your cost. You've got plenty of that.

Information Inventory

What reports, lists, studies, articles, checklists, top ten lists, survey information, or other information do you have now that prospects and customers might be interested in receiving?

_____

_____

_____

_____

Hook Audit

What hooks from other companies have you noticed in direct mail, advertisements, or commercials or on Web sites?

_____

_____

_____

_____

Hitting Your Target Market

1. What article or white paper titles are appealing to your target market?

_____

_____

_____

_____

2. Would your hooks be best offered with direct mail, in advertisements, in commercials, on Web sites or through all of these vehicles? Discuss your plans here:

_____

_____

_____

_____

3. How will you fulfill the request for anything offered by your hook?

_____

_____

_____

_____

Day 19-Summary

- You have to be different to be heard; the prospect must be hooked by you.

- Response rates increase, feedback increases, and general contact increases because of using a hook.

- A prospect who takes the hook is giving you permission to follow up and market more to him or her.

- Hooks attract attention to you and your business.

- A memorable hook attracts attention to you, what you are saying, and your business.

- A tagline can be a hook.

- The hook on a Web site makes it interactive.

- Hype is not a hook. Even though you want to appeal to the basic instincts of curiosity, desire, and convenience, overexaggeration is a turn-off.

Aha! Moments:

> Next-Level Springboards, Notes, To-Do's, etc.

Sanity Check

❏ Is this too much or not enough activity?

❏ Am I comfortable with the processes described here, the workload, and the implementation?

❏ Will the expected outcomes take me to a new level?

DAY 20

Sunday	Monday	Tuesday	Wednesday	Thursday	Friday	Saturday
	1	2	3	4	5	6
7	8	9	10	11	12	13
14	15	16	17	18	19	20 ✔
21	22	23	24	25	26	27
28	29	30				

Public Relations

P R IS SHORT FOR "PUBLIC RELATIONS." These two words are very descriptive. "Public" indicates a widespread audience. "Public" generally means everybody. "Everybody," however, is not an efficient target market. A good target market is defined, by your set of specifications that describe your target, yet still public. You actually want a relationship with your public target market, but no one talks about public target market relations (PTMR), so we will stick to public relations for our general description.

The goal of PR is top-of-mind awareness.

Day 20 in *Guerrilla Marketing in 30 Days* describes what the public wants to hear: a good story. Good PR tells a good story. The better the story, the better the acceptance by the public and the better your relationship with the public. The better the relationship, the better your chance of earning public understanding and acceptance and the easier it is to get the word out about you, your company or organization, and your products or your services. If the story is especially appealing to those who could be your clients, then you could have a PR home run, which will open many doors for guerrilla marketing and selling.

150

What Do I Publicize?

Seventy percent of what is published in newspapers is the result of a press release. Press releases are used to communicate news to media outlets. The press release states the who, what, where, when, and why of your news. The key word here is news.

PR Idea Generator

1. What events are happening within my company and/or industry this week, this month, the year?

- _____
- _____
- _____
- _____

2. What current events and/or events in the news can be tied to my business, product, service, or people?

- _____
- _____
- _____
- _____

3. What new products or services are planned for introduction or launch?

- _____
- _____
- _____
- _____

4. What opinions do I express strongly as an expert that would serve as news or that could benefit others?

- _____
- _____
- _____
- _____

5. What surveys have I done that produced results that would be news to the public?

- _____
- _____
- _____
- _____

6. What events can I produce to generate attention—contests, celebrity appearances, tent sales, celebrations, educational seminars, demonstrations, etc.?

- _____
- _____
- _____
- _____

Once you have answers to the above idea generation questions, you then can develop the topic of your press releases.

What Will I Send?

There are many right ways to craft news for your business. This news, communicated in the form of a press release, will get published or aired.

There is definitely a knack to writing a newsworthy press release, even though the ultimate goals are usually awareness and promotion. If you provide reporters and editors with news that appeals to their readers, you'll gain instant credibility and be on your way to forming a valuable PR relationship.

A Good Press Release Starts with a Good Headline

The headline is the one thing more than anything else that can dramatically improve the results you are getting from all your marketing.

This means that by improving your headlines you will get more attention and awareness.

David Ogilvy, author of _Ogilvy on Advertising_ and founder of the agency that bears his name, stated, "On the average, five times as many people read the headlines as read the body copy. It follows that unless your headline sells your product, you have wasted 90 percent of your money. ... Since headlines, more than anything else, decide the success or failure of an advertisement, the silliest thing of all is to run an ad without any headline at all—'a headless wonder.'" The same applies to a press release.

John Caples, author of *Tested Advertising Methods* and famed copywriting guru, stated, "Inquiry returns show that the headline is 50 to 75 per cent of the advertisement. So, selling punch in your headline is about the most important thing." The same applies to your press release.

Headline Tester

1. What headlines really catch your attention in the target publications or stations?

_____

_____

_____

_____

_____

Now circle the one that really grabs you!

2. What statements can you use as headlines for your press release topics/subjects?

_____

_____

_____

_____

_____

3. How can you now make the statement headlines above, more attention getting, flowery, descriptive, urgent, snappier, or informative?

_____

_____

_____

_____

_____

Five-Part Press Release Template

You can do this yourself.

Part 1: Headline

Insert headline here from previous exercise.

_____

Part 2: First Paragraph

Describing who, what, where, when, and why starts the press release in the first paragraph.

Example

Ashland, KY: Premier Therapy & Health Centers, a leading provider of Physical Therapy and named as "Best in the Tri-State" four years running by the Herald Dispatch Readership, announces the addition of new state of the art equipment to treat herniated and degenerative back discs without surgery. The equipment, the DRX 9000 is designed, in treatment, to gradually relieve neural compression often associated with lower back pain. The process has been proven to relieve pain by enlarging disc space, reducing disc space, strengthening outer ligaments to help move herniated areas back into place, and reversing high intra-discal pressures through application of negative pressure.

Your Turn:

Part 3: Second Paragraph

The last paragraph of your press release contains contact information: name, phone number, e-mail address, and Web site URL. This is in case an editor, reporter, or producer wants to contact you for more information or an interview.

Example

Marion Stevens, President of Reliable Mortgage Brokers, Inc. states that, "With people earning over a million dollars in a lifetime, its astonishing that only 4% of Americans will retire financially stable and comfortable. With paychecks really being promissory notes to home mortgages, credit card debt and bills, saving money is out of the question for most wage earners. We are committed to help families climb the steps to debt freedom. Our new Debt Rolldown Plan is proven and will do that."

Your Turn:

Part 4: Third Paragraph

Example

An eight-night cruise with the theme of the hit NBC show will sail from New York to the Caribbean on Sept. 26, after a bon voyage party in Manhattan with a send-off from Donald Trump.

Your Turn:

Part 5: Fourth Paragraph

The last paragraph of your press release contains contact information: name, phone number, e-mail address, and Web site URL. This is in case an editor, reporter, or producer wants to contact you for more information or an interview.

Example

Al is a sought after speaker on guerrilla marketing, business networking and opportunity in addition to being a featured marketing and PR expert for numerous website publications including the online version of Entrepreneur Magazine and the small business panel for USA Today. He is the owner of The Ink Well, a commercial printing company in Wheaton, IL, the principal of Market for Profits, a marketing consulting and coaching firm in Naperville, IL as well as a contributing marketing columnist for Quick Printing Magazine. Al can be contacted at al@market-for-profits.com or through the Market For Profits Web site of www.market-for-profits.com.

Your Turn:

Article Marketing Is Also Effective PR

Writing about how to do something or offering a perspective is always of value to readers. Writing articles gives you instant credibility. Submitting articles for print or for the Internet (Web sites or electronic publication) provides another good chance to get your name out into the public at no cost. Articles don't have to be long; they just need to be informative. The best articles for your target market readers are ones in which you share your experiences, offer your wisdom, tell a story, or provide some type of checklist or top-ten list or tips list. Determine your area of expertise and write about it.

Brainstorming Article Topics

Think of article topics related to your company, organization, product, service, or, best of all, the solution you have to offer to your target market.

Examples

1. Seven Mistakes People Make When Choosing a Financial Planner
2. The Hottest Trends in Home Decor
3. 15 Ways to Get All The Money You Want With Little or No Work
4. Cashing in On The Junk In Your Basement
5. A Little Kindness Means a Bigger Bank Account

Circle your favorite one.

Possible article topics for you

1. _____
2. _____
3. _____
4. _____
5. _____

Now rank them in order of priority for you.

Article Draft Generator

What questions are relevant to your article topic?

Example

What are the biggest challenges my target market is having?

Your Turn

1. _____
2. _____
3. _____
4. _____
5. _____

6. _____

7. _____

8. _____

9. _____

10. _____

Three-Part Article Template

You can do this yourself.

Part 1: Introductory Paragraph

Example

Last week I was interviewed by a radio station about something related to The Apprentice Television station. This week I have interviews lined up about the marketing of the new Harry Potter book. When Federated and May Department stores announced their merger I offered myself to the media as a marketing expert to comment on the potential name change of Marshall Fields to Macy's. You can do the same. Not with these exact stories but with something related to the media; something related to what's current in the news.

Your Turn:

Part 2: Answer the Questions Generated Above

Now answer the questions you generated in the above exercise. You can either restate the question in the body of your article or just write the answers.

Example for One Question

A publicity campaign should begin with a master plan. The more newsworthy you make your company, the more coverage you'll get. And publicity will earn credibility that advertising just can't buy. Your goals should be uniqueness, timeliness and top-of-the-mind awareness. With publicity and visibility, your company profile raises and your client and prospect level rise as well. One successful story about your company resulting in free publicity is advertising worth hundreds and thousands of dollars.

Your Turn to Answer Your Questions (do not include the numbers)

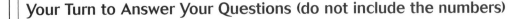

Part 3: Contact Resource Box

In the last paragraph, put the same information as you did in the last paragraph of your press release template above. This is information to enable editors, reporters, and readers to reach you for additional information or for an interview.

Example

Al is a sought after speaker on guerrilla marketing, business networking and opportunity in addition to being a featured marketing and PR expert for numerous website publications including the online version of *Entrepreneur Magazine* and the small business panel for *USA Today*. He is the owner of The Ink Well, a commercial printing company in Wheaton, IL, the principal of Market for Profits, a marketing consulting and coaching firm in Naperville, IL as well as a contributing marketing columnist for *Quick Printing Magazine*. Al can be contacted at al@market-for-profits.com or through the Market For Profits website of www.market-for-profits.com.

Your Turn

To Whom Will I Send PR Information
(Article/Press Release)?

Now that you know what you want to publicize, you have to know to whom to send your PR information. Find the publications or channels that people in your target market read, view, or listen to. Phone each and ask for the title of the person you are targeting. (See below.) This, then, is the beginning of your press contact or media database. Approach this deliberately. It's OK to start sending your news to just a few contacts. Your database of press contacts will then build after that. Many reporters, editors, and producers prefer e-mail.

Targeting Formula

1. What publications are read by my target market?

_____

_____

_____

2. What radio/TV programs are related to my news (talk, news, business, specific genre and formats, etc.)?

_____

_____

_____

3. Who is the right person at each publication or station?

Publisher _____

Editor _____

Feature Editor _____

Genre Editor _____

Feature Reporter _____

Reporter _____

Producer _____

Talent/Host _____

Other Contact _____

Target Formula Bonus Question

1. Where have I noticed my competitors in the media?

Publication: _____ Topic: _____

Editor/Reporter: _____ Comments: _____

PR Synergy

What else can you do with your press release or article, whether it got published or not?

- Post on your own Web site (see www.market-for-profits.com media room)
- Post on other Web sites
- Use in an e-mail correspondence or campaign
- Use in a direct mail piece to prospects and customers
- Hand out on sales calls
- Include in information kits
- Stock in take-one brochure rack at your place of business or office
- Include in your invoices and other mailing to customers
- Include in your bill payments to vendors
- Other _____
- Other _____

PR Checklist

❏ Do I have an idea for a press release planned for at least once a quarter?

❏ Do I have enough ideas to issue a press release every other month?

❏ Am I keeping a database of PR contacts as I learn about them and meet them?

❏ Am I regularly sending out articles for reprint and publication?

❏ Am I limiting my press releases to one page?

Day 20—Summary

- "Public relations is the management function that evaluates public attitudes, identifies the policies and procedures of an individual or an organization with the public interest, and plans and executes a program of action to earn public understanding and acceptance," according to Public Relations News.

- PR means getting the word out to the "public target market."

- Businesses and business owners become known in their fields of concentration through public relations and the associated media exposure.

- For small businesses, entrepreneurs, and guerrilla marketers, PR is most common and most efficient in newspapers.

- A new PR vehicle has emerged recently in the form of online PR.

- Seventy percent of what is published in newspapers is the result of a press release.

- Put yourself in the editor's shoes and the reader's shoes when developing PR material.

- PR is not promotion. Editors and producers hate promotion. They love news.

- If you provide reporters with news that appeals to their readers, you'll gain instant credibility and be on your way to forming a valuable PR relationship.

- Sending out a press release on a regular basis is key to keeping your name in front of your target market.

- Establishing relationships with local reporters and editors will enhance your opportunity to turn your newsworthy ideas into published news.

Aha! Moments:

Next-Level Springboards, Notes, To-Do's, etc.

Sanity Check

❏ Is this too much or not enough activity?

❏ Am I comfortable with the processes described here, the workload, and the implementation?

❏ Will the expected outcomes take me to a new level?

DAY 21

Sunday	Monday	Tuesday	Wednesday	Thursday	Friday	Saturday
	1	2	3	4	5	6
7	8	9	10	11	12	13
14	15	16	17	18	19	20
21 ✔	22	23	24	25	26	27
28	29	30				

Marketing Calendar

EFFECTIVE GUERRILLA MARKETING EMPLOYS an assortment of weapons. Guerrilla marketers aren't expected to have photographic memories; therefore, organization and prioritization of marketing is a must. This "must" takes shape in the form of a marketing plan. The visual sequence and chronology of a marketing plan's implementation is a marketing calendar. This visual is just like the useful information provided in the Farmers' Almanac.

Calendars and almanacs are normally based on astronomical events. Guerrilla marketing calendars are based on your marketing events and actions. They include your timetable for initiating and executing them.

A guerrilla marketing calendar assists you in launching your marketing vehicles in a way that can drive you to your marketing goals in a structured and well-thought-out manner.

By using a marketing calendar effectively, you will be able not only to effectively coordinate all your marketing efforts, but also to effectively budget for all of your marketing ventures.

A marketing calendar can keep you on track, ensuring that you are using every opportunity that you have to market without lapsing in your efforts. A marketing calendar can help prevent yo-yo marketing: marketing aggressively when sales are low and marketing less aggressively when sales are high.

Inventory of Events and Dates

1. Make a list of key industry events.

_____   _____

_____   _____

_____   _____

_____   _____

2. Make a list of key dates for your company (anniversary, new product introduction, reorganization, relocation, etc.).

_____   _____

_____   _____

_____   _____

_____   _____

3. Are there any promotional or marketing tie-ins between the two sets of dates listed above?

_____   _____

_____   _____

_____   _____

_____   _____

Marketing Weapons Listing

List all your marketing weapons, marketing initiatives, and marketing activities

_____   _____

_____   _____

_____   _____

_____   _____

_____   _____

_____   _____

Timing Planner/Estimator

1. Estimate timing for each initiative, e.g., a press release every other month, chamber newsletter ad once per quarter, a direct mail postcard to a particular target segment once a month for six months.

_____   _____

_____   _____

_____   _____

_____   _____

_____   _____

_____   _____

2. Take the timing for each initiative and place it visually on a 12-month calendar. Refine the timing from there. Use your favorite spreadsheet here.

   Write in your completion date here when done: _____

Important: Put on your calendar "marketing calendar review dates" to grade marketing, revisit initiatives, and revise your calendar accordingly.

Day 21—Summary

- The visual sequence and chronology of a marketing plan's implementation is a marketing calendar.

- A guerrilla marketing calendar assists you in launching your marketing vehicles in a way that can drive you to your marketing goals in a structured and well-thought-out manner.

- A marketing calendar not only effectively coordinates all of your marketing efforts but also effectively budgets for all of your marketing ventures.

- The marketing calendar is a management tool.

- All marketing initiatives and actions can be place on a calendar.

- Another benefit to a marketing calendar is that it prevents bunching of activities or excessive periods of inactivity.

Aha! Moments:

Next-Level Springboards, Notes, To-Do's, etc.

Sanity Check

❏ Is this too much or not enough activity?

❏ Am I comfortable with the processes described here, the workload, and the implementation?

❏ Will the expected outcomes take me to a new level?

DAY 22

Sunday	Monday	Tuesday	Wednesday	Thursday	Friday	Saturday
	1	2	3	4	5	6
7	8	9	10	11	12	13
14	15	16	17	18	19	20
21	22 ✔	23	24	25	26	27
28	29	30				

Other Marketing: Coupons, Speaking, and Contests

Some of the weapons described on this day are the only ones used by some guerrilla marketers—and quite successfully at that.

Coupons

WHEN YOU THINK "COUPON," you basically think certificate of redemption. Guerrillas use coupons mostly in newspapers and magazines. Sometimes they include a coupon in fliers and handbills.

Coupons are viable marketing vehicles for increasing product sales. Couponing is another way to commit people to brands that interest them most. They provide value in the form of price discounts. They are best used in the spirit of guerrilla marketing in conjunction with other supporting marketing. Coupons are best used to create a short-term blip in traffic for a particular establishment, focused around one simple product or service.

Speaking

One of the best ways for potential clients to find out about you, your company, and your products and services is for you to tell them, for them to hear information straight from you. You are your best marketing vehicle. You can do this through general conversation or presentations. Speaking to groups is nothing more than a large conversation. Speaking to groups is powerful marketing and efficient marketing.

Contests

The primary purpose of the contest is to gather as many entrants as possible. The cost for you to get these names is the cost of what the contest winner wins. This price for a targeted, permission-based list is a small investment compared with the potential return. That's the way all guerrilla marketing should be.

Coupon Attack Planner

1. What products or services of yours are best suited for a coupon offer?

_____

_____

_____

2. When a prospect presents that coupon for redemption, in what ways can you upsell him or her? For example, "Because you are redeeming your coupon today, you qualify for this special offer of ...."

_____

_____

_____

3. How will you present a coupon to your target market? In print? Included in packaged products? Included in invoices and statements? Online?

_____

_____

_____

"Will Speak for Marketing"

1. Visit www.nsaspeaker.org and review professional speakers by the subject or topic of expertise that is consistent with you or your company.

   Done: _____

2. What subjects or topics of expertise are consistent with yours?

   _____

   _____

   _____

3. What value could you offer in a presentation that is related to your business or industry or area of expertise?

   _____

   _____

   _____

4. To which groups or associations do your target market prospects belong? List contact information for each.

   _____

   _____

   _____

   _____

   _____

5. What "system" can you invent that makes for a valuable presentation or speech?

   _____

   _____

   _____

"And the Winner Is ..."

1. What kind of contest can you hold that you can build publicity around?

_____

_____

_____

2. How can you publicize the announcement of a contest?

_____

_____

_____

3. What other businesses and organizations hold contests for which you can donate your products or services, as the prize for the winner?

_____

_____

_____

4. What database tracking system will you put in place to compile contact information for contest entrants?

_____

_____

_____

5. How will you market to your new database after the contest? Through what communication vehicles? With what messages?

_____

_____

_____

_____

6. Once you determine a winner, how will you publicize the result?

_____

_____

_____

Day 22—Summary

- Coupons are viable marketing vehicles for increasing product sales. Couponing is another way to commit people to brands that interest them most.

- The lifetime value of a customer using a coupon is well worth the coupon cost as that customer returns to buy more products.

- Coupon marketing is very conducive to measurement.

- One of the best ways for potential clients to find out about you, your company, and your products and services is for you to tell them, for them to hear information straight from you in the form of public speaking.

- Speaking to groups is powerful marketing and very efficient marketing.

- Speaking to a group is not direct selling.

- The primary purpose of a contest is to gather as many entrants as possible.

- All entrants to a contest are permission-based prospects to whom you can market after the contest.

- Contests don't have to be fancy; they can be publicized and will generate word-of-mouth buzz.

Aha! Moments:

Next-Level Springboards, Notes, To-Do's, etc.

Sanity Check

❏ Is this too much or not enough activity?

❏ Am I comfortable with the processes described here, the workload, and the implementation?

❏ Will the expected outcomes take me to a new level?

DAY 23

Sunday	Monday	Tuesday	Wednesday	Thursday	Friday	Saturday
	1	2	3	4	5	6
7	8	9	10	11	12	13
14	15	16	17	18	19	20
21	22	23 ✔	24	25	26	27
28	29	30				

Online Marketing, Part 1

IN THIS DAY AND THE NEXT, we will scratch the surface of online marketing and give you some weapons that you can use if you are involved in something undergoing rapid and ongoing change. Even if not, there are still online marketing fundamentals that tie into guerrilla thinking and will produce the guerrilla results that you are coming to expect.

> Technology should be used in guerrilla marketing. Never have we been at the point that we are today in using technology in marketing.

Not to sound like a guerrilla broken record, but defining your objectives and having a plan is as important for online marketing as it is for all other marketing. You want a Web site, but what are you going to do with it? You have e-mail. Do you communicate effectively with it and to the right people? These are the types of things you want in your plan and the types of questions you want to answers to in order to go forward with success.

Make sure you don't try to do too much with your online marketing. Online marketing still takes finite resources to implement and maintain. Develop only what is pertinent and comfortable for you, your business, and your resources. Your Internet business strategy should be an extension of your company's current marketing strategy and well integrated with marketing done offline.

Online marketing is more than a Web site and e-mail. Choosing what is right for your business and the marketing of your products and services and what people in your target market like, want, and need will determine your online course of action.

Internet Action Steps: Before the Site

1. Visit competitors' Web sites. What do you like, what you not like from a customer's point of view?

Competitor Site No. 1

_____

_____

_____

Competitor Site No. 2

_____

_____

_____

Competitor Site No. 3

_____

_____

_____

Competitor Site No. 4

_____

_____

_____

The Web Site

1. Solicit input from your customers about your site. How can you make it more friendly, valuable, and useful? What do they like and what don't they like?

_____

_____

_____

_____

2. How would you judge your site on the following criteria on a 1–10 scale, where 1 is poor and 10 is excellent? Give your reasons for rating it that way.

Your site is interactive: _____

_____

_____

_____

Your site is a resource for customers and prospects: _____

_____

_____

_____

You have a reason for surfers to return to your site: _____

_____

_____

_____

It's easy to respond or buy from you: _____

_____

_____

_____

3. Answer the following questions about your site.

What value does your site provide?

_____

_____

_____

What is your online and/or Web site hook?

_____

_____

_____

Do you follow the principle of AIDA—attention, interest, desire, action? What parts of this are strong on your site and what parts would you like to improve?

_____

_____

_____

Is there a place for people to sign up for free information on your site?

_____

_____

_____

Do you have a way to capture the e-mails when people sign up for your information?

_____

_____

_____

"Build It and They Will Come—Not!"—Marketing Your Site

1. What key search words would you want associated with your Web site for search engine searches?

_____ _____ _____

_____ _____ _____

_____ _____ _____

2. What offline marketing is available to drive traffic?What offline marketing is available to drive traffic?

_____

_____

_____

3. Do a search on key words related to your business and see how the results rank your competitors and what they are doing.

Competitor Site No. 1

_____

_____

_____

Competitor Site No. 2

_____

_____

_____

Competitor Site No. 3

_____

_____

_____

Competitor Site No. 4

_____

_____

_____

4. Visit a pay-per-click search engine (like searchmarketing.yahoo.com, www.miva.com, and www.goclick.com) and see what costs are associated with click-throughs. Also see what keyword search quantitative information is available.

_____ _____ _____
_____ _____ _____
_____ _____ _____
_____ _____ _____
_____ _____ _____
_____ _____ _____

5. Reconcile against your key words and determine your breakeven point on using this marketing weapon.

_____
_____
_____

Linkage, Linkage, Linkage, Linkage

1. What businesses would be logical for you to trade links with?

_____
_____
_____

2. What do your customers want to link to from your site?

_____
_____
_____

3. What links are on your competitors' Web sites?

_____
_____
_____

Day 23—Summary

- Defining your objectives and having a plan is as important for online marketing as it is for all other marketing.

- Online marketing still takes finite resources to implement and maintain.

- Your Internet business strategy should be an extension of your company's current marketing strategy and well integrated with marketing done offline.

- Online marketing is more than a Web site and e-mail.

- Understanding what information people in your target market want or need is paramount when determining Web site content.

- Getting listed in search engines is still one of the best ways to drive qualified, targeted traffic to Web sites.

- Pay-per-click search engines allow you to bid on keywords related to your site. If you win the bid, your site will be ranked highest for that keyword.

- Reciprocal links with other businesses or organizations are another highly successful way to get traffic to your Web site.

- Your Web site is an advertising medium that has more in common with the telephone than with a brochure. Interactivity is the key to Web site success.

- Online marketing should be integrated with all other marketing activity.

- Becoming a trusted resource of high-quality information is of tremendous value to you, your business, and your position in the marketplace.

Aha! Moments:

Next-Level Springboards, Notes, To-Do's, etc.

Sanity Check

❑ Is this too much or not enough activity?

❑ Am I comfortable with the processes described here, the workload, and the implementation?

❑ Will the expected outcomes take me to a new level?

DAY 24

Sunday	Monday	Tuesday	Wednesday	Thursday	Friday	Saturday
	1	2	3	4	5	6
7	8	9	10	11	12	13
14	15	16	17	18	19	20
21	22	23	24 ✔	25	26	27
28	29	30				

Online Marketing, Part 2

IN DAY 23 YOU READ THAT TECHNOLOGY in marketing starts with two basic weapons: e-mail and a Web site. Both should be treated as process-oriented marketing, not event-oriented weapons. It's time to apply marketing that does something with your site or with your customers to get them to visit your site. Visiting the site is only half the battle.

> Conversion from visitation to sales is the ultimate goal of all Internet marketing.

Now we will start with e-mail marketing and follow it with other weapons within Internet marketing that will aid in achieving your conversion goal.

E-Mail

E-mail is the most popular online activity and use of the Internet. Just look at your own e-mail activity. E-mail has exploded in size and use. It has also exploded in abuse. Guerrillas operate within ethical parameters in all marketing, especially e-mail. Do not send spam messages.

For most small businesses, permission-based e-mail marketing campaigns are the most memorable and cost-effective way to reach new and existing customers. The key is to do it right and do it with permission. This marketing can consist of e-mail newsletters or targeted personalized messages.

E-Mail Targeting Exercise

1. How often do you want to communicate to your targeted e-mail list?

_____

_____

_____

2. How will you obtain your permission-based targeted list?

_____

_____

_____

E-Mail Message Exercise

1. What messages will you use (content)?

_____

_____

_____

2. What creative subject lines have caught your attention in e-mail messages?

_____

_____

_____

3. How can you adapt these subject lines for your use?

_____

_____

_____

4. What hook or free information can you offer in your e-mail marketing?

_____

_____

_____

5. What is your follow-up system? What will you do when you get a response to your e-mail marketing?

_____

_____

_____

6. Do you have an auto-responder system to deliver and manage your e-mail marketing? If not, what system is compatible with your usage and budget?

_____

_____

_____

Driving the E-Zine Vehicle

1. Collect e-zines on subjects you like and your competitors' e-zines, if you can. List the site URLs or titles.

_____

_____

_____

_____

_____

_____

2. What components of each e-zine do you like the most and which ones will appeal to your customers and prospects?

_____

_____

_____

_____

_____

_____

_____

3. What will be the format, title, and content of your e-zine?

_____

_____

_____

_____

_____

_____

4. To whom will you distribute your e-zine and how?

_____

_____

_____

_____

_____

Online PR Machines

1. Visit some online PR sites, like www.prweb.com, and review other companies' PR. As part of this exercise, type "online PR" into a search engine to see what sites come up.

_____

_____

_____

2. To what online sites is it logical for you to send your online press release?

_____

_____

_____

3. Type "article submission" in a search engine and find sites to distribute your online feature articles to.

_____

_____

_____

"A Serious Thing Happens on the Way to the Forum ... and Back"

1. What discussion forums cover your area of concentration or interest?

_____

_____

_____

_____

_____

_____

_____

_____

2. What information can you contribute to these forums to position yourself as a resource?

_____

_____

_____

3. How often will you visit the forum?

_____

_____

_____

Day 24—Summary

- Conversion from visit to sales is the ultimate goal of all Internet marketing.

- E-mail is the most popular online activity and use of the Internet.

- For most small businesses, permission-based e-mail marketing campaigns are the most memorable and cost-effective way to reach new and current customers.

- E-mail marketing can be a tool for branding, direct response, and building customer relationships.

- Your e-mail signature—your name, contact information, and URL—can drive interested prospects to your Web site.

- You need an e-mail recipient's permission before you can send him or her an e-mail marketing your product or service. Do not send spam.

- Auto-responders are programs set up to automatically respond to e-mails when triggered.

- Auto-responders ensure a consistent and frequent communication tool to touch prospects the sufficient number of times.

- The number-one reason people are online is because they desire and need information. The popularity of e-zines is based on that need.

- An e-zine is a great mechanism to keep in touch with customers and prospects.

- An online press release is a low- or no-cost way to spread the word about your news.

- Putting PR information on your Web site is another use for online PR.

- Online press kits are becoming more and more popular.

- Discussion forums online enable users of a Web site to interact with each other, exchanging tips or posting conversation and information that is useful to each other.
- Online marketing should be integrated with all other marketing activity.

Aha! Moments:

Next-Level Springboards, Notes, To-Do's, etc.

Sanity Check

❏ Is this too much or not enough activity?

❏ Am I comfortable with the processes described here, the workload, and the implementation?

❏ Will the expected outcomes take me to a new level?

DAY 25

Sunday	Monday	Tuesday	Wednesday	Thursday	Friday	Saturday
	1	2	3	4	5	6
7	8	9	10	11	12	13
14	15	16	17	18	19	20
21	22	23	24	25 ✔	26	27
28	29	30				

Trade Shows and Expos

HAVE YOU EVER VISITED A TRADE SHOW or business expo and walked past a booth of non-guerrillas, chitchatting away in social mode? Do you think these people understand the word "trade" in "trade show"? Do you think these people are great socializers? Do you think they are more proud of how pretty their booth looks? Chances are, in a non-guerrilla world, the answers to these three questions are no, yes, and yes.

A trade show is an event at which goods and services in a *specific industry* are exhibited and demonstrated. The key words here are "specific industry." If the specific industry of the trade show is made up of members of your target market, a trade show may be an effective marketing weapon for you. These shows are also known as *exhibitions*, *expos*, and *trade fairs*.

One of the first considerations is determining whether a trade show is an appropriate venue for you and your business. This is best understood by reviewing your target market. Targeting is a common theme with any of the guerrilla marketing weapons. This one is no different.

A trade show venue brings together people with similar interests, ideas, and challenges. Gearing your efforts to these people's needs makes trade show marketing effective and profitable.

Planning for a trade show is no different from knowing your destination when you leave on a family vacation. Not doing so leaves your experience and success to chance. You, as a guerrilla, want more of a sure thing; therefore, planning is a must.

Trade Show Research

1. Visit a trade show before exhibiting at one, preferably one in your industry or one similar. List the ones you visit and the primary focus of each:

_____

_____

_____

2. At what trade shows do your competitors exhibit?

_____

_____

_____

3. What are the major trade associations in your industry? Which ones have trade shows or exhibitions?

_____

_____

_____

4. What are the major trade associations in your customers' industry? Which ones have trade shows or exhibitions?

_____

_____

_____

5. Which trades shows are appropriate for you and how many people attend each one?

_____

_____

_____

Trade Show Planner

1. What objective would you state for trade show exhibiting? Think back also to the purpose of your marketing.

_____

_____

_____

2. What do you want visitors to do as a result of stopping by your exhibit?

_____

_____

_____

Pre–Show Countdown

1. What will your message and/or announcement be to your customers and prospects prior to a trade show?

_____

_____

_____

2. What will make your exhibit/booth different? What one thing do you want prospects to remember about your presence at the show?

_____

_____

_____

3. What follow-up system can you put into place?

_____

_____

_____

4. Will you have any special offers for your products and services?

_____

_____

_____

5. What giveaways will you offer? Information? Promotional items? Samples and other items?

Information:

_____

_____

_____

Promotional items:

_____

_____

_____

Samples and other items:

_____

_____

_____

The Trade Show Holy Grail

Who will coordinate the trade show reservations, planning, execution, and details and what resources are needed to do so?

_____

_____

_____

_____

_____

Day 25—Summary

- A trade show is an event at which goods and services in a specific industry are exhibited and demonstrated.

- A trade show is effective marketing if the specific industry or focus of the trade show is made up of members of your target market.

- Your trade show plan should include your objective for exhibiting.

- Your objective at a trade show is to make contact with current customers, meet new prospects, and get leads.

- Other reasons for exhibiting at a trade show include expanding your identity, awareness, presence, and visibility and introducing a new product or service.

- Have a trade show marketing plan that includes your objective, theme, message, promotions, marketing vehicle used, follow-up plan, and budget.

- You should do your event marketing plan with publicity in mind.

- Other pre-show marketing planning that must be done is deciding on which vehicles will be communicating your marketing message at the show.

- Trade show participants are attracted to exhibits that are unique.

- Trade shows open doors and pave the pathways to building strong business relationships with customers, prospects, distributors, the media, and other partners in your industry.

- You should follow up immediately with those most interested in your offerings, within two or three days of the show.

- Great presentation and display and great pre- and post-show communication will ensure a successful use of trade show marketing.

Aha! Moments:

Next-Level Springboards, Notes, To-Do's, etc.

Sanity Check

❏ Is this too much or not enough activity?

❏ Am I comfortable with the processes described here, the workload, and the implementation?

❏ Will the expected outcomes take me to a new level?

DAY 26

Sunday	Monday	Tuesday	Wednesday	Thursday	Friday	Saturday
	1	2	3	4	5	6
7	8	9	10	11	12	13
14	15	16	17	18	19	20
21	22	23	24	25	26 ✔	27
28	29	30				

Newsletters

ONE OF THE BEST VEHICLES TO communicate news and information to the business public (your customers and targeted prospects) is the aptly named newsletter.

> Newsletters have four times the readership of traditional ads. Newsletters are perceived to be more credible and believable than ads. Newsletters have a longer shelf life than ads and are passed around for others to read.

Newsletter communication comes in many forms. Regardless of the form or the context, you are generally providing your prospects and customers with valuable information. You are extending your relationship with those who read your newsletter. You are making another guerrilla attempt to maintain and improve your top-of-mind awareness with your target market. You are paying attention to those most likely to buy from you. Paying attention can be a competitive advantage.

Who's Doing What and What's Doing What?

1. If you have a newsletter now, what response do you get?

_____

_____

_____

_____

2. Save newsletters that you receive. What do you like about them?

_____

_____

_____

_____

3. What don't you like about them?

_____

_____

_____

_____

4. Do they inform, persuade, or entertain you?

_____

_____

_____

_____

Plan Your Newsletter

1. What is the objective of your newsletter?

_____

_____

_____

_____

2. How many pages will your newsletter be?

_____

_____

3. How will you distribute your newsletter? How will you use it?

_____

_____

_____

_____

4. Will your newsletter be a self-mailer or will it be inserted into an envelope for mailing?

_____

_____

_____

5. Does it make more sense to offer a one-page electronic newsletter (www.onepage-newsletters.com)?

_____

_____

6. In what ways will you use your newsletter?

_____

_____

_____

_____

Putting Ink on Paper

Is your newsletter print-friendly? What suggestions/recommendations did you get from a printing professional or a designer?

_____

_____

_____

_____

_____

_____

_____

Day 26—Summary

- One of the best vehicles to communicate news and information to the business public (your customers and targeted prospects) is a newsletter.

- With a newsletter, you are generally providing your prospects and customers with valuable information. You are extending your relationship with those who read it. You are making another attempt to maintain and improve your top-of-mind awareness with your target market reader.

- Newsletters provide an opportunity to inform your customers and prospective customers of your opinions, facts, and persuasions on a wide variety of matters.

- Newsletters are usually produced on a regular basis in multi-page format for the purpose of communicating newsworthy information, education, company updates, special offers, and points of interest for your prospects.

- Newsletters work only when they are distributed to your customers on a consistent basis.

- Newsletters can also be used as handouts to prospects and customers and as backup material for any media interviews.

- Free tips in a newsletter position you as an expert in your industry and show your attitude for helping others, both advantages over your competitors.

- The more uses you find for your newsletters, the more efficient your marketing will be.

Aha! Moments:

Next-Level Springboards, Notes, To-Do's, etc.

Sanity Check

❏ Is this too much or not enough activity?

❏ Am I comfortable with the processes described here, the workload, and the implementation?

❏ Will the expected outcomes take me to a new level?

DAY 27

Sunday	Monday	Tuesday	Wednesday	Thursday	Friday	Saturday
	1	2	3	4	5	6
7	8	9	10	11	12	13
14	15	16	17	18	19	20
21	22	23	24	25	26	27 ✔
28	29	30				

Marketing Budgets

A QUESTION OFTEN ASKED BY SMALL business owners, professionals, and other entrepreneurs is how much they should spend on marketing. They are really looking for a number that represents a percentage of their total sales revenue.

Asking this question is almost like asking how much you should eat. The answer depends on how hungry you are and what nourishment you need.

Guerrillas are hungry for market share; therefore, marketing expenditures should be higher than average.

One thing for sure is that guerrillas plan where to spend their money and how much to spend. They do not plan their business, check to see what money is left over, and spend it on marketing. That is gnitekram allirreug—guerrilla marketing backwards. You should view your marketing budget as a major business investment, just like a piece of equipment, just like a key employee, and just like the overhead over your head. No one has ever claimed a business success by marketing with what was left over. Certainly no guerrilla has ever one so.

One of the biggest marketing budget concerns is where to spend the money available. Budget items to consider include advertising on the radio and TV and in newspapers and magazines; Web sites; marketing communication materials; PR; newsletters; and direct sales. The key to marketing budgeting is deciding what items to spend on, their priority, and the amount available from the company till. Once you've made those decisions, you have the basics.

The List and Your Marketing Report Card

1. What marketing items did you spend money on last year or so far this year?

_____

_____

_____

_____

_____

_____

_____

_____

_____

_____

_____

What worked and what didn't? Grade each item on the above list A, B, or C or from 1 to 10.

2. What would you repeat and how much would you budget for it?

_____

_____

_____

_____

3. What is your marketing vehicle with the highest return on investment?

_____

_____

_____

_____

What Will I Spend? What Can I Spend?

1. What new products or services do you plan on introducing?

_____

_____

_____

_____

2. What marketing will you need to budget for these?

_____

_____

_____

_____

_____

_____

_____

_____

_____

_____

3. What other expansion or improvement plans do you have that will need marketing (people/facility/product/service)?

_____

_____

_____

_____

What if?

1. How would you spend 10 percent of last year's sales dollars on next year's marketing?

_____

_____

_____

_____

_____

_____

_____

_____

_____

2. What marketing ideas or weapons can you use that cost nothing?

_____

_____

_____

_____

3. What will be your periodic marketing budget review process?

_____

_____

_____

_____

4. Put review dates on your marketing calendar.

_____

_____

_____

_____

5. Based on the above information, the planned marketing expenditures can be summarized as follows:

_____

_____

_____

_____

_____

_____

_____

_____

_____

_____

The total expenditures amount to: _____

Day 27—Summary

- Good marketers plan where to spend their money and budget how much to spend.

- Part of the marketing budgeting process is understanding where you got bang for your buck, what worked and what didn't, and where marketing dollars can be spent most effectively.

- Spend money on marketing that works.

- Understanding marketing expense patterns of previous years will help you formulate future requirements.

- Marketing budgets aren't expenses regardless of what your accounting intuition tells you. They are expenses only if they don't work.

Aha! Moments:

Next-Level Springboards, Notes, To-Do's, etc.

Sanity Check

❏ Is this too much or not enough activity?
❏ Am I comfortable with the processes described here, the workload, and the implementation?
❏ Will the expected outcomes take me to a new level?

DAY 28

Sunday	Monday	Tuesday	Wednesday	Thursday	Friday	Saturday
	1	2	3	4	5	6
7	8	9	10	11	12	13
14	15	16	17	18	19	20
21	22	23	24	25	26	27
28 ✔	29	30				

Plan Execution and Implementation

In *7 HABITS OF HIGHLY EFFECTIVE PEOPLE*, Stephen Covey states, "All things are created twice. There's a mental or first creation, and a physical or second creation to all things. ... You have to make sure that the blueprint, the first action, is really what you want, that you've thought everything through. Then you put it into bricks and mortar. Each day you go to the construction shed and pull out the blueprint to get marching orders for the day. You begin with the end in mind."

Guerrilla Marketing in 30 Days is your blueprint. It's now time to visit your guerrilla construction shed, grab the tools that you have developed over the past 27 days, and go to work.

As stated in *Mastering Guerrilla Marketing,* "The plan is your guide and you are the master."

Marketing strategies typically don't fail in the mental creation. They fail in implementation. You haven't come 28 days to fail. Failure is not an option. That's why we devote this whole day to the physical creation (implementation) that Mr. Covey refers to. Ensuring the effective implementation of marketing strategies is one of the highest- impact ways to marketing success.

Start with the End in Mind

Write a success story of your successful plan implementation. (Think with the end in mind here.)

_____

_____

_____

_____

_____

_____

_____

_____

_____

_____

_____

_____

_____

_____

_____

_____

"After Further Review ..."

1. What review system will you use to monitor implementation of your marketing initiatives?

_____

_____

_____

_____

2. Are there any employees, partners, or associates who can be project or initiative champions or mini-project leaders?

_____

_____

_____

_____

3. Put review dates on your marketing calendar.

_____

_____

_____

_____

_____

_____

4. State your intentions to someone. Whom did you tell and what did you tell?

_____

_____

_____

_____

_____

_____

5. Hire a marketing coach to hold you accountable and to guide you through your plan implementation. Investigate who would work best for you.

_____

_____

_____

_____

Day 28—Summary

- A successful marketing plan will never produce results without successful execution.

- Marketing implementation is simply managing marketing activities.

- The heart of the implementation of a marketing plan is the execution, the actual "doing" of the planned marketing activities.

- Accountability is a good marketing habit.

- Poor implementation is usually traced back to lack of follow-up and tracking.

- If you have to have something done and you simply don't have the people, talent, or resources internally, then hire someone to do whatever you need done.

- Once you have the marketing plan, you must follow up and respond to changes in the market, changes in customer demands, competitive influences, technological advances, and new ideas.

- Mastering guerrilla marketing requires taking action. Taking action is implementation.

- Now is the time to start implementation.

- You are in charge of your own actions.

Aha! Moments:

Next-Level Springboards, Notes, To-Do's, etc.

Sanity Check

❏ Is this too much or not enough activity?

❏ Am I comfortable with the processes described here, the workload, and the implementation?

❏ Will the expected outcomes take me to a new level?

Additional Notes

Sunday	Monday	Tuesday	Wednesday	Thursday	Friday	Saturday
	1	2	3	4	5	6
7	8	9	10	11	12	13
14	15	16	17	18	19	20
21	22	23	24	25	26	27
28	29 ✔	30				

Expansion/New Markets/New Income Streams/New Products

WITHOUT PROGRESS OR ADVANCEMENT, there is stagnation. In the business world, this leads eventually to demise.

Why must businesses grow? Why must they prosper? What if they get comfortable doing what they do best? Why do they need to pursue opportunities? Why must they expand? Why must they develop new products and services? The answers to these questions lie in the fact that businesses get complacent.

> Complacency is a killer. Complacency kills because things change all around you. Customers' demands change, economics change, and competition dynamics change. We have heard over the past 28 days how guerrillas are responsive to change.

One of the ways to overcome complacency, ensure company growth, and be responsive to the many market changes and influences is to develop new products, product improvements, new services, new streams of income, and new markets.

Progress and advancement are the lifeblood of guerrilla companies. If you are not seeking progress and advancement, you stand to face stagnation, complacency, and eventual demise. This challenge, in no uncertain terms, represents what lay people categorize as a problem. When thinking like a guerrilla, any act or process of solving a problem is a solution. Solutions are market opportunities. True, there are times when pursuing opportunities doesn't work out, but in the total scheme of things all successful companies have succeeded because they went looking for an opportunity, spotted one, and acted upon it. They progressed and advanced as a result. They saw the chance and went for it. There was a chance that their problem—whether it was lack of growth, lack of market share, or lack of anything else—would be solved if only the opportunity sought panned out. Thinking along these lines will deliver your future success.

Blue-Sky Thinking

1. Do you have the potential to serve global markets?

_____

_____

_____

_____

2. Can you expand geographically beyond where you are serving now?

_____

_____

_____

_____

3. Does that take more locations?

_____

_____

_____

_____

4. What other resources would be required to do this?

_____

_____

_____

_____

Ideal Customer Profile

1. Do you need to change, tweak, or re-evaluate your profile of your ideal customer?

_____

_____

_____

_____

2. Are there other customer profiles that you could target with your current offerings?

_____

_____

_____

_____

Bundling Exercise

1. What new products and services can you bundle with current products and services?

_____

_____

_____

_____

2. Can you bundle your products and services with someone else's to offer more value to the combined group of customers?

_____
_____
_____
_____

Thinking Strategically

1. Are there pricing, distribution, or service strategies that can be developed around what you are currently doing?

_____
_____
_____
_____

2. What strategies in these areas can be developed that are radically different from what you are currently doing?

_____
_____
_____
_____

3. What is your Baby Gap, your Snakelight, or your Double Stuf Oreo opportunity?

_____
_____
_____
_____
_____
_____
_____
_____

Day 29—Summary

- One of the ways to overcome complacency, ensure company growth, and be responsive to market changes is to develop new products, product improvements, new services, new streams of income, and new markets.

- Companies creating new wealth aren't simply executing better; they're radically changing the rules of the game and they're creating situations, environments, products, services, markets, and experiences that produce opportunities.

- Progress and advancement are the lifeblood of guerrilla companies.

- Sometimes progress and improvement takes the form of repackaging, refining, re-development, or turning something old into something new.

- How you can re-create your product or service in such a way as to stand out and affect customers and prospects in a new and different way is the improvement question at hand.

- Opportunity or expansion comes in the form of developing new streams of income.

- Many companies use product diversification to create multiple streams of income.

Aha! Moments:

Next-Level Springboards, Notes, To-Do's, etc.

Sanity Check

❏ Is this too much or not enough activity?

❏ Am I comfortable with the processes described here, the workload, and the implementation?

❏ Will the expected outcomes take me to a new level?

Additional Notes

DAY 30

Sunday	Monday	Tuesday	Wednesday	Thursday	Friday	Saturday
	1	2	3	4	5	6
7	8	9	10	11	12	13
14	15	16	17	18	19	20
21	22	23	24	25	26	27
28	29	30 ✔				

New Plan—The Next 30 Days and Beyond

WHAT NEXT? THIS IS A QUESTION that every business, every guerrilla marketer, and you should ask everyday. Where do you go from here? How can you improve upon what you have done? What more successes do you want?

The answers to these questions are your renewal factor. They contain the impetus behind your re-engineering. What are you doing every day to re-engineer yourself? These answers are the stepping stones to that proverbial "next level" that you want to reach.

At the end of these 30 days, you have completed action steps and developed plans. The paramount question at hand is "What would you do differently over the past 30 days if you had to relive them, if you were starting this book all over again?"

This time around you will know your strengths and your weaknesses. You will have a feel for what works and what doesn't. This knowledge and this experience leads to better focus.

With a foundation in place, you now can think beyond your current scale. How do you make your guerrilla marketing efforts pay off bigger, be more productive and more profitable?

217

With a foundation in place, you can now learn and apply more. What have you learned about yourself in the past 30 days? What were some roadblocks along the way? What resources could you use more of? These are common questions to follow-up planning. Although you are asking these questions on Day 30, they should be ongoing follow-up questions.

The Next 30 Days ...

1. What is next? Where do you go from here? Write out your thoughts on these questions.

_____

_____

_____

_____

2. How can you improve upon what you have just done in the past 30 days?

_____

_____

_____

_____

Your Definition of Success

What more marketing successes do you want?

_____

_____

_____

_____

_____

_____

_____

_____

Looking Within

1. How do you make your guerrilla marketing efforts bigger, more productive, and more profitable?

_____

_____

_____

_____

2. What have you learned about yourself?

_____

_____

_____

_____

3. What were some roadblocks that came up during your 30 days of guerrilla marketing?

_____

_____

_____

_____

4. What resources can you use more of? How can you get more of these?

_____

_____

_____

_____

What's Next?

1. List your top three guerrilla marketing priorities for the next 30 days. Just three. You will have more than three, but for focus and this action step, list just the top three.

   _____

   _____

   _____

2. Who can you recommend this book to?

   _____

   _____

   _____

3. What other guerrilla titles would you like to see? E-mail me: al@allautenslager.com.

   _____

   _____

   _____

Day 30—Summary

- Your starting point for the next 30 days is the answer to the question of what you would do differently over the past 30 days of learning if you could relive them.

- With a foundation in place, you now can think beyond your current scale.

- Marketing is changing even as you are reading this and even as you are planning new activities.

- Integration of systems, whether marketing or other, will be a point of emphasis as companies strive to be more efficient and more effective.

- Customers will become more interested in their total experience in dealing with you, not just a transaction.

- "There has never been a better time than right now to give wings to our dreams through marketing. There has never been a better way to market than with the insights and attitudes of the guerrilla."

Aha! Moments:

Next-Level Springboards, Notes, To-Do's, etc.

Sanity Check

❏ Is this too much or not enough activity?

❏ Am I comfortable with the processes described here, the workload, and the implementation?

❏ Will the expected outcomes take me to a new level?

To order *Guerrilla Marketing in 30 Days*, other Guerrilla Marketing books by Jay Conrad Levinson, or other books and products by Al Lautenslager, please visit:

www.market-for-profits.com or e-mail: **al@allautenslager.com**